write here write now

Foreword

by

PUBLISHED BY THE PRESS SYNDICATE OF THE UNIVERSITY OF CAMBRIDGE
The Pitt Building, Trumpington Street, Cambridge, United Kingdom

CAMBRIDGE UNIVERSITY PRESS
The Edinburgh Building, Cambridge CB2 2RU, UK
40 West 20th Street, New York, NY 10011–4211, USA
10 Stamford Road, Oakleigh, VIC 3166, Australia
Ruiz de Alarcón 13, 28014 Madrid, Spain
Dock House, The Waterfront, Cape Town 8001, South Africa

http://www.cambridge.org

First published 2001

Printed in the United Kingdom at the University Press, Cambridge

Typeface Concorde   *System* QuarkXPress®

A catalogue record for this book is available from the British Library

ISBN 0 521 79963 5 paperback

Sales of this book will benefit two charities:

Home-Start
which supports young families in crisis

Write Away
which is a penfriend club that enriches the lives of children
and adults with disabilities, their families and carers, through facilitating
and encouraging writing and other forms of communication

Home-Start	Write Away
2 Salisbury Road	1 Thorpe Close
Leicester LE1 7QR	London W10 5XL
Reg. Charity no. 289169	Reg. Charity no. 1059701

CONTENTS

FILM / TV SCRIPTS

    *   NATIONAL WINNER

  **   NATIONAL RUNNER-UP

***   TEACHERS' NATIONAL AWARDS FOR IMPROVEMENT WINNER

Foreword

by
The Rt Hon. David Blunkett, MP
Secretary of State for Education and Employment

The **Write Here, Write Now** competition was designed to support the National Literacy Strategy and complement the work of teachers in raising standards of writing. Learning to read and write well is essential to get the best possible start in life. That is why we introduced the Literacy Strategy – to help children develop their skills, and improve their chances of success in their working lives as well as in school. Teachers are achieving excellent results through the Literacy Hour and standards are rising.

I hope all the pupils who took part in the competition found it helped them with their writing. Sir Alan Ayckbourn, Roger McGough, Phil Redmond and Jacqueline Wilson set them quite a challenge. But I'm sure the competition was also interesting and exciting. Obviously not everyone could win, but everyone could have fun taking part. I hope all those who took part found that learning is not just hard work, but is also enjoyable. I certainly enjoyed reading the winning entries and I'm sorry that I couldn't get through all 33,521! I was very impressed by the quality of the writing and the imaginative and creative ways in which the children developed the opening lines. I did not envy the judges. I know they had a very difficult job in choosing the winners.

I hope the competition inspired children to continue writing creatively, and not just at school. Who knows, some of them may become the Jacqueline Wilsons or Roger McGoughs of the future. But we can all be writers, and we can all improve our writing skills. That is why we are continuing the emphasis on writing in the Literacy Strategy, and why we will be launching another competition next year.

I am grateful to everyone who helped to make this year's competition such a success: all the pupils and teachers who took part; the four authors who helped to make it so interesting; the regional and national judges; the celebrities who gave their support; and of course, Cambridge University Press, the Disney Channel and Mattel Interactive, who generously donated the prizes.

I hope you enjoy reading the winning stories, poems and scripts in this book. It is indeed a celebration of children's writing.

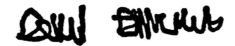

29 November 2000

INTRODUCING THE WORK OF THE PRIZEWINNERS

All over England through the summer term of 2000, Year Four and Five pupils were encouraged to write stories, poems and scripts for this competition. Deliciously enticing openers provided by celebrity writers set the scene, drawing our young writers into themes, ideas and scenarios that gave them something real, something intriguing and entertaining, to write about. The selection included here is just the tip of the iceberg; from the mountains of entries, regional judges chose those pieces which showed qualities of imagination and a grasp of technical form that made them stand out from the rest.

The writers are children in the middle of their junior years who, having learnt the basics, are now acquiring a writer's knowledge of the genre, exploring what the written word can offer to those who are prepared to grapple with its exacting difficulties. The judges were looking for well-crafted pieces with that spark, that something, which makes the reader sit up and take notice.

To whet your appetite, each of the four sections which follow – stories, plays, poems, film/TV scripts – have introductions, giving a snapshot of the winners in each genre. The opening lines by our celebrity writers are given too.

As you will see from the list of contents, one piece from each genre was chosen as a national winner and there was also a runner-up story and poem. In addition, keep a look out for the Teachers' National Awards for Improvement winners in the story and poem categories. As part of the competition, teachers were given the opportunity to nominate a pupil who showed the most significant improvement in their writing. There are three winners in this special category.

The entries can be viewed on the competition's website (www.writehere.org.uk). This is particularly important if you want to read the full play, TV and film scripts, which for reasons of space appear edited in this book.

The children's writing has, in general, been left unaltered but occasional changes have been made to aid clarity and fluency of reading. For consistency, punctuation has also been standardised throughout the book, except in the poems, where the winners' own punctuation has been kept.

STORY

JACQUELINE WILSON WROTE ...

You'll never guess what happened yesterday! I thought it was going to be another dreary old Monday. We overslept so that meant we were all rushing round trying to do six things at once. I don't recommend eating toast and honey while struggling into your school uniform. You end up feeling sticky all day long.

Squirt and I had a small discussion – okay, heated argument – about the ownership of a grey school sweatshirt. We were still fighting over it when we got to school, each tugging on an empty sleeve. Squirt tugged hardest, crammed the sweatshirt on like a hat and ran for it across the playground, the sleeves waving like twin trunks.

I was going to get into trouble for being late – and for not wearing a school sweatshirt. (Squirt is so mean, I know that sweatshirt is mine. It's got all the little ink tattoos I doodled one day when I was in an artistic mood.) However, as things turned out, no one realised I was late. It didn't matter that I wasn't wearing full school uniform. Everyone was so distracted I could have gone to school in my pyjamas and no one would have noticed.

This was because ...

INTRODUCING THE STORIES

What a wonderfully enticing opener to a story! We start with a distraction – is it realistic, fantastic, the beginning of an action-packed adventure? – and a familiar space, the school playground (not to mention Squirt!). But, perhaps surprisingly, given the everyday reality of the opening passage, all but three of the winners zoomed off, full of life and fun, into fantasy.

In the exceptions, Fern's vivid description of a mural that appears mysteriously on the playground wall evokes a work of art; but who painted it, and will they get into trouble? James, in an excitingly realistic account, has an Army tank crash through the school wall, threatening everyone inside. Helen's Manic Monday, with its anarchic set of horrid siblings, might have been real, but we can be forgiven for doubting it! And Elyse's spooky story about a deserted school leaves the reader quite unnerved – until all is explained!

In his piece, Tom sets up a computer-like space game, pitting terrifying green orks against a horde of New Delhi wizards, and Philippa brings mayhem to school in the shape of a mob of circus animals; it takes a modern-day pied piper to get rid of them. Lauren-Lucy slips down a hole in the playground and meets Henry the Eighth, with whom she and Squirt have an improbable conversation about tights and tunics!

Some of the stories have a moral at the heart of them. Emily describes a hideous monster who thrives on dirt, pollution, noise and fighting: he's a lord of misrule. The problem is, how to get rid of him? Both Jessica and Sarah have a similar theme: in what way should you respond to strange-looking aliens who appear in your school – with instinctive hostility, or with a practical sort of kindness?

Jacqueline Wilson cast a story-spell on that playground. It's time for you to step into it ...

No Normal Day

This was because everyone was staring at the centre of our playing field. I ran up to join the crowd (being naturally nosy), to find a huge circle made of burnt grass. All the kids were being pushed back by lots of men wearing Army clothes. Other people were arriving in vans, lorries, tanks and even helicopters.

That was enough for me, I was having a bad enough hair day without the wind from a helicopter making it worse. I left the hustle and the bustle and made my way into my classroom. It wasn't that I wanted to take a peep at our spelling test for that day, but it just happened to be lying on Miss Preece's desk! Just as I was reaching out for it, I heard a noise; it seemed to be coming from the art cupboard.

Imagining stray cats or escaped frogs, I carefully opened the cupboard door. Staring back at me were three (yes, that *was* three) gold eyes. Opening the cupboard door further (I was always the brave one) I saw two weird looking kids. On further inspection, I saw they were not kids at all, they were still weird looking but they definitely weren't human. With blue skin and round heads, they had three fingers on each hand and three toes on each foot. Did I forget to say that they each had three arms and legs? This all went very well with their three eyes!

I was amazed! For as long as I could remember I had been fascinated by the thought of 'aliens'. ET had become my favourite film once I stopped being terrified of it! I didn't run away like my brain was telling me to, because they had friendly, worried looking eyes (all six of them). Without actually talking, they made me understand that they had come to earth to take a picture of our Millennium Dome back to their planet for their Universe Exhibition. A small mistake on their map had led them to be stranded on the Westbury Farm School playing field.

They explained that they had panicked when they saw hundreds of grey uniformed humans rushing towards them screaming at the top of their voices, so they had made their spaceship invisible and had taken cover in a nice quiet, dark place – the art cupboard.

This was too much for one person, even when that person was me. I rushed back to the field and grabbed Squirt. Dragging her into the classroom, I poured out my story. Squirt stared at the aliens and gulped. "H-ow do you d-do?" she asked in her best Mummy manners.

The aliens quickly explained to both of us that they needed to get back to their ship as it would only stay invisible for another ten minutes.

Having watched 'X-Files' a couple of times (Mum and Dad were out, and the baby-sitter thought we were watching 'You've Been Framed'), we knew we had to help them before the FBI (the English version) would capture them and do horrible tests and things.

Having covered Squirt from head to toe in blue paint with big circles of black felt over her eyes (with a slit so she could see), she went running round the field. With cameras flashing, all the people started to chase her while she led them round the back of the school.

My new friends and I quickly ran to the burnt grass circle. One of the aliens began to glow and suddenly a small, gleaming spaceship appeared. In their strange way, they told me how grateful they were to us both and hoped that Squirt wouldn't get into too much trouble.

"Don't worry about her," I said confidently, remembering our earlier battle with the sweatshirt. "She can look after herself!"

Having promised they would get in touch, the aliens said goodbye and flew off to Greenwich to get their picture.

Helping Squirt scrub off the blue paint in the girls' toilets, we agreed the day had been anything *but* a dreary old Monday!

By Jessica Kukielka, aged 9
Eastbury Farm JMI and Nursery School, Northwood
East of England Winner

Manic Monday

This was because everyone was staring at something out of the window whilst our distraught teacher, Miss Derry, who wore glasses and floaty skirts and was a bit dim, rushed about shouting, "Sit down children, please sit down!" in a hoarse voice, tripping over her skirt in a very undignified way.

I pushed my way to the window and gaped at what I saw. Outside, someone had parked an extremely long stretch limo. I watched excitedly, hoping it was someone really famous, but the only people who got out were a family of seven who didn't look at all famous.

As the limo drove away I noticed a sign on the back saying 'LIAMS HIRE LIMOS'. 'What a way to make an entrance,' I thought.

An hour later, I wished I had never gone to school that morning. The new kids were absolute horrors! You couldn't go round a corner without having paint chucked over your head or beetles put down the back of your top. They all had mean faces and dark eyes like their parents.

The headmaster had introduced them in assembly and then their parents had scarpered. Several teachers had rushed home declaring they had the flu and didn't want to give it to the children.

The last straw came when the headteacher tripped over a banana skin, purposely put there by a 'horror'. He yelled so loudly I called an ambulance.

This only left Miss Derry, who was screaming by now ... just as a school inspector walked through the door!

'It must be a surprise visit,' I thought, seeing the confused look on Miss Derry's face. "Quick," I said to Miss Derry, "I have an idea. You welcome the inspector, I'll get everyone back to their classrooms."

I rounded up four of my friends and told them to take a class each. With great difficulty we got everyone back to their classrooms. Some we had to push in and hold the door until they stopped pulling to get

out. Then I explained my plan. "We can turn it into a big drama session and the inspector will never know!"

I then went to spell out the details to Miss Derry, who agreed wholeheartedly, probably not capable of anything else at that minute, the state she was in.

The next hour went by in a flash. The 'Drama Project' as we called it, was a success. We acted out everything that had happened during the day and Miss Derry stood by with a sort of feeble smile on her face, watching the new kids act their parts perfectly. The inspector left after break, looking satisfied, and Miss Derry was almost fainting with relief.

Then I noticed that Squirt was missing. I also noticed that the 'horrors' had very devilish grins on their faces. After searching for half an hour we found him tied upside-down in one of the boiler houses.

I got back my sweatshirt, found it wasn't mine, and then it was home time. Miss Derry said I deserved an award (I bet it's a new school sweatshirt!).

I can't wait to see what will happen today!

By Helen Tulloch, aged 10
Tickton CE Primary School, Beverley
Yorks and Humberside Winner

Academic Animals**

This was because the school had been invaded by circus animals that were visiting our town. Everyone was mesmerised by the exotic creatures who had taken over our school.

I first noticed a monkey hanging from the blackboard, chalk in his left hand, scribbling on our ABC frieze. My attention was taken away by screams of laughter from the assembly hall. A hyena, situated on our stage, was shrieking at the top of his voice to the sound of the choir singing 'He's got the whole world in his hands.' Our music teacher's ability to play had declined due to extreme circumstances.

I then walked into the gym to view a band of seals playing ball on their noses. My next recollection was the sight of a giraffe with his head stuck through our new roof. There were elephants in the kitchen eating bread and buns and squirting water at any unsuspecting person who was unlucky enough to obstruct them. No one dared to go near our headmaster's room – a lion had decided it was the best place for a nap and was snoring loudly for all to hear.

The whole school had been taken over by the mob of circus animals.

Our normally calm staff were in panic. "Come to the hall" was the cry heard throughout the building. We made our way into the hall. Not in the usual orderly two by two manner, but in a complete muddle. The children stood in groups around the hall looking to the staff to begin their plan. Mr Horsewhip, the headmaster, just stood with his mouth open not uttering a word. Miss Flute, the music mistress, squealed. Her voice was usually soft and sweet but she could not hit one correct note today. The PE teacher, Mr Flip, just circled round and round making us all feel dizzy. My form teacher, Mrs Trip, a normally level-headed lady, was running with a butterfly net trying to catch the hyena who was still on the stage.

It was obvious that no adult could solve the mayhem in our

school. Apart from the animal sounds the school was now in silence. What could be done? Who could come up with a good idea? I looked about but all I saw were puzzled faces and shrugged shoulders. Tommy Tadpole, the smallest boy in the school, was gazing up through the hole in the roof. His expression was blank as normal (unfortunately Tommy is not the brightest of children, he never wins prizes or shines at sports). He began to hum and then to whistle. It was annoying at first but suddenly I noticed the giraffe lowering his head to examine Tommy more closely.

Tommy was oblivious and wandered into the playground, with the giraffe in hot pursuit. Elephants, monkeys and seals streamed behind the giraffe. The hyena had come down from the stage and he too was following Tommy.

Mrs Lippy, the lollipop lady, had witnessed the fiasco and had informed the circus. Wagons and trailers assembled in the car park. Tommy whistled his way up the ramp with animals following. Even the lion, who had woken to the sound of whistling, was safely loaded onto a trailer.

Tommy was a hero. He and his family were awarded a free trip to the circus.

By Philippa Breeze, aged 10
Chester-le-Street CE
Junior School, Durham
North East Winner
** National Runner-up

Clean-up

This was because all the children were backing away from the school entrance, white-faced and gobsmacked. For some reason nobody could speak. Suddenly, out of nowhere, a huge moat flooded around the school. As if being knocked out of a trance, everyone screamed and jumped back, a look of horror on their faces. Squirt, I could see, was having trouble with huge rats who were addicted to my school sweatshirt. (I don't think she really wanted it after all.)

Suddenly with a flash of green light a gigantic troll king appeared with huge, lumbering arms and a pig's snout for a nose. His skin was warty and green with boils popping up all over his body. I screamed in unison with the rest of the school. Then the troll started whispering and everyone fell silent to listen.

He said, "We are here to help the world stay a dirty place and not be clean, for our food is dirt and pollution. We love noise and enjoy fighting as much as we love smell. Our community is dying out because of school rules and 'No Litter in the Corridor' signs. This school is fairyland for us and we hope never to leave it. Unless you work out our weakness we will not be stopped and shall be getting ever stronger and ever smellier!"

Then he disappeared in a puff of green smoke.

I suddenly got it; we had to be quiet to get rid of the trolls. We also had to pick up rubbish and keep clean.

I climbed to the top of the huge red climbing frame and shouted over everyone's racket, "Stop, be quiet, don't you understand, the only way to stop them is to be quiet and clean up." I watched as they were quiet and stared up at me, a guilty look on their faces. Then I shouted at the top of my voice, "Who's with me?"

At those words everyone cheered and Squirt started a chant, "Clean up, clean up." People joined in and even the teachers had a few words. Then Squirt joined me on the climbing frame. "Goodbye

trolls, here comes our plan, you'll be knocked off, to your gran." I smiled at her. Squirt can make up rhymes so easily.

Suddenly, the whole school was on their knees picking up litter in silence. The moat faded. Somebody shouted, and it came into view again.

'Bother!' I thought. 'If this isn't done soon the troll will come back and make noise.'

All of a sudden there was an almighty crack and everyone thought it would ruin the plan, but it didn't. What had happened? I looked around and the moat had gone. Then I heard a high-pitched scream.

"NOOooooooooo, NOOooooooooooo." The voice faded away. Everyone cheered as if they wanted the sky to fall down. But only I saw the vivid outline of a hunch-backed figure going through our big black gate and into the school just down the road. At least that's cleaned up for now.

By Emily Arch, aged 9
Belmont Primary School, Chiswick
London Winner

What a Weird Day

This was because, in my rush to get to school on time, I hadn't noticed that the streets around the school were empty and, when I thought about it, so was the playground, except for me and Squirt.

I made my way to the classroom. All the corridors were very quiet. Suddenly I jumped out of my skin! Someone or something was running along the corridor towards me! I turned round quickly, hardly daring to look – but it was only Squirt!

"Everyone is missing from my class, even Miss Roberts," he said.

"Same here," I said.

"I'm scared, Lily, what's happening?"

Together we crept along the corridors, but every classroom was the same – not a sign of life. There was something very strange going on. Our school should be full of shouting children, but there wasn't a sign of anyone, not even Jeremy Simpson who was the school swot and who was always at school well before anyone else and who always stayed behind after school to help Mrs Jobes or to read in the library. What was going on?

I tried to think of all sorts of answers but they all sounded stupid. Squirt thought perhaps everyone had been beamed up by spacemen and taken to their planet where they would be forced to work in the salt mines. Stupid boy! I think he's been watching too much 'Star Trek' or 'Alien Men from Mars'.

I told Squirt that I thought we should make our way home and tell Mum all about it. It was ten-thirty by now and Mum would be back from Gran's where she went each morning to help her get dressed and give her some breakfast.

Our house was only round the corner, more or less, from school, so Squirt and I ran for home. We decided not to stop, no matter what.

As we reached the school door we heard a voice in the distance. It sounded strange. Squirt turned round.

"It's a monster," he screamed. "It has big eyes and funny skin. Just run!"

And we did – and didn't stop until we got to our back door.

"Mum, Mum," we shouted.

"Where have you two been?" asked Mum.

"Mum, Mum, everyone has disappeared, even Mrs Roberts!" said Squirt. "And a strange alien chased us down the corridor. But we were too fast for it."

"A monster? An empty school? Let's just calm down. Why were you two at school on a Sunday morning? And had you both forgotten that Mr Jacks the caretaker was going to fumigate the school? He was probably your monster – in a protective suit!"

I looked at Squirt and Squirt looked at me. Sunday? No wonder everywhere was empty!

"You silly gooses," said Mum, "I thought you got enough of school Monday to Friday without going in on a Sunday as well!"

We all laughed. But I hope no one saw us going in on the wrong day.

By Elyse Oxley, aged 10
Holy Family RC Primary School, Barrow-in-Furness
North West Winner

New Delhi Wizards

This was because a horrible green-skinned creature was sitting looking awe-struck in the middle of the playground. The creature was sitting there because when he attempted to warp through a warp hole it went wrong and he ended up in the playground.

I joined the huddle around the creature, next to Squirt. Everyone was holding their noses, as the pong from the creature was immense. As I got closer to the creature, I saw its skin was wrinkled – from a distance it looked smooth. The large monster had a stuck-up nose with a rusty ring through it. Below its nose it had a horrible row of sharp teeth and curved horns from its mouth which reached its pointy ears.

I thought I had seen the monster before. Suddenly, I remembered my little sister's monster book. The creature was an Ork! Our headmaster came outside and ordered us to move away. He was looking very shaken. We all backed off from the Ork and stood at the edge of the playground.

Just then three police cars screeched to a halt and out came all of the officers. The Ork, seeing them, sprang to its feet and out of nowhere produced an axe! Two of the girls fainted and our teacher, Mrs Cropford, leant against the wall looking shaken. One policeman raised a pistol and shot. The bullet hit the Ork's tough hide and ricocheted off across the playground.

Everyone was scared, even Bill Richmond, the biggest bully in school, was frozen. The Ork was a bit slow to react, but soon it realised what was going on. It advanced on the policeman, axe waving in one hand and a long, curved scimitar in the other. As it charged across the playground it screamed, "Aloy cumber nit wok alow necly econ!"

All of a sudden, a dark portal appeared on the playground wall. The Ork didn't take any notice but out popped about thirty more Orks! In sheer panic the policemen jumped in their cars, but they were attacked by the vicious mob of Orks. Soon the cars were beaten smouldering wrecks on the road. The Orks then returned to the playground and closed up on us. Just as they were in striking range they turned around and there was standing a New Delhi wizard – the only thing Orks are afraid of!

The Orks rapidly funnelled into the building. They crashed up the stairs into a classroom. As they surged through the rooms, they knocked tables flying and smashed through the doors. The wizard followed then, all of a sudden, he stopped dead and bellowed, "Hard Ork bone, turn to stone!"

At that bellow, three Orks turned to stone. Then hundreds more wizards appeared next to the wizard's side. The Orks stood mortified, their clumsy green feet didn't move. The wizards together all yelled, "Hard Ork bone, turn to stone!" All of the Orks turned to hard grey stone. The wizards instantly disappeared in a puff of purple smoke without a trace.

Today, if you go to the school, at the entrance there are two stone Orks. The others were sent to museums, but some are still lost in portals.

By Tom Hardman, aged 10
Bosvigo School, Truro
South West Winner

Gorgeous Graffiti

This was because as soon as I walked (actually flew) through the school gates, I realised things weren't what they should be. Normally, Jamie and his Pokémon princes (as he would call them) would be patrolling round looking for new cards. Michelle and Daisy would be prowling round the boys, vying for attention, and the king and queen of football, David and Denise, would be jumping up and down hugging each other after a goal. But today things were extremely different.

I pushed my way through the crowd to see what all the fuss was about. Roger stood staring like a shrivelled tomato, all hot and sweaty. But standing next to him, Jamie was grinning as if he had just won the last card to fill his Pokémon collection. I looked all around the motionless playground, I could have heard a pin drop! It was almost like a huge magnet attracting everyone's gaze, and following it I found myself in front of an artist's wonderful work. It was a gigantic picture of a garden. Gorgeous graffiti was all over the walls, on the windows and a massive beautiful butterfly covered the hall wall.

Teachers came running out of the classrooms, mouths wide open like giant road diggers. Mrs Scribblewobble (as we would call her because of her hectic scribbling on the blackboard and her going round the classroom like a bouncy ball from pupil to pupil) was a sight to see. She stared in amazement, as did the other teachers, at the golden daffodils, at a silver pond with a statue's mouth trickling with glistening water. You could see an early morning's dew on a neatly knitted spider's web. A colossal oak in the middle of the garden holding its young seeds of new life in its bronze rough palms. Other insects flying over the pond and a six-foot-high dragonfly with its

fairy-like wings and blue scales wrapped around its body. A frog, looking almost lifelike, with its slimy skin and slippery green back.

Rumours spread and people said that those responsible for this would get extremely told off. An immensely loud bell rang and everyone stood silent. The teachers hauled us in like a herd of sheep. Doors slammed behind us and we were wondering what was going to happen. I thought the painting was rather good. Mr Handsome (we didn't make that name up – trust me he's not *that* handsome) marched into the hall behind us. Everyone was tense. It was a normal assembly with normal teachers, but we were puzzled. Mr Handsome told us a normal story as usual. However, when we were stumbling out again, he caught us by surprise. There were police officers at every door checking our hands for tell tale signs. If you think about it, spray paint doesn't come off that easily.

The guilty culprits slouched into Mr Handsome's office. We tried listening through the door. (Even the teachers showed curiosity!) Suddenly the door opened and the three culprits all had smiles on their faces. Apparently they had all got congratulated for making the school a brighter place. So another day's work done. Being late wasn't such a bad thing after all. Sammy, the chief artist, is now teaching me to paint!

By Fern Bowles, aged 10
Fordingbridge Junior School, Fordingbridge
South East Winner

The Seymour Attack*

This was because the digger had finally arrived! It was enormous. A huge mass of yellow metal. They weren't *that* excited to see a digger, you understand ... I mean who hasn't seen one of those? It was *what* the digger was doing!

The school yard was to have a new adventure playground, courtesy of Mr Rex the head – we call him 'Dino'. I started to shout the news to my best mate, Charlie, who was late and looked like she'd slept in her uniform, when Squirt screeched.

I turned to see Squirt being teased by two big kids (*they* thought they were big anyway!). They'd grabbed the honey-flavoured sweatshirt. Squirt jumped for it and fell into the freshly dug hole. You know what it's like with pesky kid sisters – I could hardly stand by and watch, could I? So, me being me, I jumped straight into the hole too, just as the dreaded Miss Seymour marched on to playground duty ... and 'see more' she normally did!

We landed on a cobbled floor.

"Gee wizz, that was a bumpy ride, where are we?" I spluttered.

"Who knows?"

"Hey, look, he's going to that fancy dress party Mum was on about."

"Can't see Dad wearing those silly tights," Squirt giggled. "Look at those fake higgledy-piggledy houses."

"They're not fake, they're real," I gasped. "T-t-t-hey're Tudor!"

"Aha, I see you've returned my tunic," the man in tights bellowed.

"You mean Squirt's smelly sweatshirt?" I stammered.

"My hunting tunic. I'm Henry the Eighth. You should be bowing."

Triple gulp!

"You draw?" he boomed, pointing to the doodles on the sweatshirt.

"Yyyes."

"What, with quill and ink?" he demanded.

"No, Sir, with gel pen. Mum got three for the price of two at WH Smith."

"Pel gen? Let me see," he ordered.

What a stroke of luck! It was in my pocket.

"That would amuse my third wife, Jane Seymour. I'll take it," Henry retorted. "She's in need of cheer. She's expecting my child any day now."

Henry glared at Squirt. "Have you brought a gift for your King?"

"Mmm, not exactly, Sir," Squirt confessed, digging deep into her pocket and bringing out a half-chewed lolly, an old bus ticket and her Pokémon cap!

"Off with her head!" Henry screeched.

Now, have you ever had a day when you wake up and wish you hadn't bothered getting out of bed? Well I definitely decided I was having one. I needed to think quickly.

"Sir," I cried, "This Jigglypuff cap is just what you need."

Henry took the cap and gave his Tudor hat to Squirt. I seized my chance. I grabbed Squirt's hand and dived for the hole. Suddenly, we found ourselves rushing through space. We landed with a thump in the playground.

"Where on earth have you girls been? Where's your sweatshirt? What are you doing with that hat? Why are you late?" thundered a voice.

Miss Seymour was not to be messed with. I tried to explain, but she was in no mood for stories – especially ones that involved the King of England!

We hurried off. Then we saw it! Standing in all its glory was the adventure playground – finished! My eyes stared in disbelief! There, hanging from the monkey bars, was the honey-flavoured sweatshirt … complete with Henry the Eighth's signature!

By Lauren-Lucy Grafton, aged 9

St Augustine's RC School, Kenilworth

West Midlands Winner

* National Winner

What Is That?

This was because everybody was staring at the front of the hall. Everyone was there: all eight teachers, Mr Spite the headmaster and even Mr Gribbs the caretaker who was usually too busy shouting at us to do any fixing or cleaning. I knew from the start that something was wrong.

I had to kneel up to see what was going on. When I saw what there was to see, I wished I'd stayed put.

A strange creature was ripping up the display board. It was definitely not one of God's creations. It had the tail of a tiger, the head of a wolf, the body of a crocodile and the feet of a badger. Its long jaws were just chewing up a painting of a Second World War soldier.

Just as I'd finished gaping at the creature's scaly body, Mr Gribbs did the most stupid thing I have ever known anyone to do in my entire life. It was even more stupid than Squirt hiding Mum's wedding ring. Our caretaker looped a piece of rope round the striped tail.

The creature whirled round to face Mr Gribbs, a paper Army tank hanging from its sharp, yellow teeth. Mrs Tracker (my teacher) hid behind the school's ancient piano.

"Come and get it then!" yelled Mr Gribbs acting calm and brave although he had gone white as a sheet. The creature just snarled, showing his sinister fangs.

The creature advanced on Mr Gribbs with slow, careful steps, saliva hanging from its mouth. Its menacing eyes glowed with anger. Mr Gribbs started to back away, but he knew he couldn't escape.

Then suddenly the creature whirled round. Mr Spite had obviously done something to annoy it. Just as the fierce creature was cornering the headmaster, a sudden movement distracted its attention. One of the reception children was walking towards it.

To our amazement, the creature didn't tear the child to pieces, it just stared. Then, an astonishing thing happened. The youngster just walked forward and started stroking the creature's head. Everyone gasped, but the strange creation closed its eyes and made a purring noise. But the child didn't stop there. He climbed up onto the spiky crocodile back and kicked the creature's shins. It galloped off with the boy still on its back.

Well, after that, the pandemonium was over. The whole school started talking. The staff were trying to think of a way to break the news to the missing child's parents.

The rest of the day was as normal as any other. Mr Gribbs and Mr Spite took the afternoon off to look for the brave child. They returned with nothing at three o'clock.

Then, while we were at assembly, the missing child walked calmly through the hall door as if nothing had happened. He didn't even talk about it.

Squirt and I walked home together, running over the events of the day. Just as we walked onto our stone path, Squirt handed me the grey sweatshirt we were arguing over that morning. "It's yours," he mumbled and ran off. I looked at the sweatshirt. It had a huge hole in one arm.

I'll kill him. I really will.

By Sarah Bovey, aged 10
Chetwynd Road Primary School, Nottingham
East Midlands Winner

The Tank ***

This was because of the strange thing in front of us. It looked like a tank and it was. The teacher told us to stay back. Squirt didn't hear her and ran to the window. It looked like a frightful, fearful giant. The other children in the class didn't know that in the tank there were live bombs and it was scaring me to death.

Squirt had shouted to me that the red flag was flying on the tank range as I chased him through the fields to school. That meant live fire practice! Now one of the tanks from the Army base down the road had crashed off the road and had smashed through the playground wall.

I started to shiver. It was like being in a bath with freezing cold ice cubes in it. Now and then the tank, which was stuck half way through the wall, would suddenly slide a few feet closer towards our classroom with a dramatic screeching. Looking out of Class Three's window we could see right down the barrel of the gun. It was pointing to the corner of the room where my desk was. I ran at the speed of light down to the hall. This was the moment of truth … or death. I felt scared and terrified. I flung myself under the table in the dining hall and screwed my eyes shut and waited.

After a while I opened my eyes slowly, one at a time. The hall was still there and Miss Plum was shouting my name. "Tim, Tim Fisher! Where are you?" Perhaps others had survived too, but why did one of the survivors have to be my dreaded old form teacher? Crawling out from under the table everything looked normal. Miss Plum saw me and grabbed my arm tight and dragged me back to the classroom.

"We have to take the register now – what are you doing under there?"

"But Miss we can't go back there, there are bombs on that tank, I know."

"Don't be stupid, boy," exclaimed Miss Plum. "The Army don't drive around here with real bombs."

Just then a tall man in an Army combat suit came round the corner. "Clear the building immediately," he barked.

When I was out of the building, the soldiers were heading in and out of the classes cautiously. I was trying to stop the tank from knocking down the classroom by shouting at the invisible driver inside. The front of the tank was an inch away from the wall. I shouted again at the tank, "Stop, stop you're smashing our school!" They must have just heard me, as the tank stopped with a jerk and a big hiss from the brakes. The door opened very slowly and out crawled a worried looking soldier.

"Wow, what a mess. Sorry kids. Our periscope jammed and I couldn't see the road."

"Have you got real bombs in there Mister?" shouted out Squirt.

"Oh no son, we pick them up at the range, you're all safe enough. Want to climb aboard for a tour?"

It was great. We spent the rest of the morning climbing all over the tank and sitting in the driver's seat until a huge truck came to pull it back onto the road. Miss Plum was all stressy and had to go and lie down in the staff room. Squirt says he wants to be a tank driver now, especially if you can go around knocking schools down!

By James Heyes, aged 9

Upham CE Primary School, Southampton

*** Teachers' National Awards for Improvement Winner

James is a wonderful example of how perseverance pays off; determined to perform to a high standard, James has worked impressively over the last year to overcome the difficulties of dyspraxia. His test scores in reading and writing are testimony to his achievement.

PLAYSCRIPT

ALAN AYCKBOURN WROTE ...

*A darkened room. **Sarah** and **Jason** enter cautiously, looking around them.*

Sarah	Now where are we?
Jason	*(Hesitantly)* I don't know.
Sarah	What do you mean, you don't know? You're the one who got us here.
Jason	All right!
Sarah	I just followed you.
Jason	You didn't have to.
Sarah	You said you knew where you were going.
Jason	I didn't ask you to follow me, did I? Why did you have to follow me?
Sarah	I ...
Jason	No one asked you, did they?
Sarah	I wasn't letting you go in on your own. That's all.
Jason	I'd have been all right. I knew what I was doing.
Sarah	Really?
Jason	Yes, really.
Sarah	Then where are we, then?
Jason	I don't know.
Sarah	Exactly.

A pause. They look around again.

Jason	We've – we've somehow got inside this game. That I do know ...
Sarah	Oh, brilliant. Even I gathered that much. But where's the game gone?
Jason	No idea.
Sarah	There should be characters, shouldn't there? Surely? There should be creatures? There should be scenery? There's nothing here at all.
Jason	Maybe we're in a part of the game where nothing much happens.
Sarah	*(Sarcastically)* And where it's pitch dark?

Jason	Right ...
Sarah	Well, we'd better go somewhere light, hadn't we? Look for someone who can tell us how to get home again?
Jason	I suppose.
Sarah	Then lead on, expert.
Jason	Er ...
Sarah	What? What are you waiting for?
Jason	If we do meet someone – they might not necessarily be friendly.
Sarah	Oh great.
Jason	They might actually attack us.
Sarah	Terrific.
Jason	Or if they're creatures, some of them – might try to eat us.
Sarah	Wonderful! Tell me, are we likely to meet anyone friendly, at all?
Jason	Oh, yes. There's plenty of them.
Sarah	Good.
Jason	Provided we can find them. They're usually hiding.
Sarah	Why are they hiding?
Jason	Well, they're waiting to be rescued, aren't they?
Sarah	I see. And who's supposed to be rescuing them?
Jason	Well, us.
Sarah	*(Resigned)* I give up. Lead on, then.
Jason	*(Uncertain)* Which way do you think?
Sarah	*(After a slight pause, pointing)* That way!

*They set off, **Sarah** in the lead. The scene changes quickly to ...*

INTRODUCING THE PLAYS

In a sense a game, be it electronic or on a board, is like a play: it has its own defined arena with a set of rules guiding its action; it may have characters (heroes and villains) and it has a forward momentum leading to an unknown conclusion. Both entertain; both, too, in their different ways, require that we get involved in unfolding events, pitting our wits against that of the games master or the playwright. It is rich material for a set of fantasy plays and our playwriters seized the opportunities it presents.

Perhaps it is not surprising that two of the most enduring board games, *Cluedo* and *Monopoly,* provide the starting point for several of the scripts. *The Murder of Doctor Black,* for instance, is the classic *Cluedo* whodunnit turned into a comedy. *Monopoly* gets transformed, merging with the possibilities of computer games. In *Jurassic Monopoly,* for instance, the children, trapped inside a computer game, encounter dinosaurs (which ones are friendly, which aren't?). The children's fate – as in several other games – is all but decided by the roll of the dice and the deal of the cards. *Hagem* has a modern (and more sinister) shopping version of *Monopoly* in which the children, in danger of having parts of their bodies nibbled away by 'cribbles', 'shoplifters', 'teeth trolleys' and 'gaps', have to rescue eight-year-old twins trapped in the game, whose self-identity is fast fading.

Other playwriters, equally adventurous, invented their own games. In *The Journey of the Block* the children get sucked into a block of light, gateway to a perilous fantasy in which they encounter a sedra (a blue water-dragon) and get lost in a maze. In *Lost in the Game* they help Haddi, a monkey, battle with the wolfmen who have kidnapped his father; but only some jewels can release him. There are battles, too, in *Game Trap,* against tigers, a crocodile and a shape shifter (where Lara Croft, no less, makes a guest appearance) and in *The Riddle of the Warehouse,* where the children not only have to pit themselves against 'bluggers' and 'gleeks' but have to solve riddles too. *Remember It's Only a Game* has an exciting quest involving an Egyptian mummy and a pit full of scorpions.

Looming over or controlling several of the games is a games master (yet another metaphor for fate in a scenario rich with them). Ben, in *Into the Future,* controls the game in which Jason and Sarah find themselves – a game which includes its own creators who have become trapped within it! And *The Murder of Doctor Black* has perhaps the ultimate in this respect: small, micro-Sarah and Jason look up at their normal, physical selves playing the game, yet both are real within their own dimensions. Such sophistication!

Many of the plays could work equally well on film, in cartoons and as computer games, for they are all rich in fantasy. Producers thinking about staging them will often find the possibilities of the theatre stage being extended to its limits, drawing on mime, lighting effects to suggest scene changes, masks, evocative but minimal props and sets. But as with all good scripts, the first impact is felt by the solitary script reader. So, read on!

The Riddle of the Warehouse

Main characters
Sarah, Jason, The Warehouse Manager, Garuda, King of the Orb

Scene 1

Jason	*(Uncertain)* Which way, do you think?
Sarah	*(After a slight pause, pointing)* That way!
	*They set off, **Sarah** in the lead.*

Scene 2

Sarah and Jason walk out of the dark room and end up on a beach with a forest behind them.

Jason	Look! Look!
Sarah	What?
	*A beam of light appears in the sand. The **Warehouse Manager** appears.*
Manager	*(Slowly and clearly)* I am the Warehouse Manager. I am here to help you.
Jason	*(Sarcastically)* Yes, and I am King Kong.
Manager	Quiet. I have to help you rescue the King of the Orb. You will need certain equipment for each game zone, which I can give you. Before I give it to you however, you will need to answer a riddle.
Jason	*(Worried)* But what if we get it wrong?
Manager	There is no need for you to know that. This is your first riddle. What is sometimes a friend and sometimes a foe?
	***Sarah** and **Jason** look thoughtful and talk between themselves.*
Sarah	We're not too sure but we think it's the sea.
Manager	Correct. Here is the equipment you will need for this level. A peashooter and a bag of salt.

	*The **Warehouse Manager** disappears.*
Jason	He's gone.
Sarah	Look over there. There's a raft. Let's use it to cross to the island.
	Suddenly a group of blood-red frogs appear on the sand.
Jason	Holy shamoly. What are they?
Sarah	I don't know, but let's kill them.
Blugger Leader	You will have to defeat us, the Bluggers, to get to the raft. If you defeat us you are worthy of the quest.
Jason	What shall we do?
Sarah	Let's use the peashooter. It's all we've got.
Jason	But what do we put in it?
Sarah	The salt, of course.
	***Jason** grabs the peashooter and loads it with salt.*
Blugger	That won't hurt me.
Sarah	Zap him!
Jason	All right, all right.
Sarah	And make sure it's on target.
	*There is a bang as the salt hits a **Blugger**. The **Blugger** shrivels and dies.*
Sarah	That was close.
	***Sarah** and **Jason** make their way to the raft, fighting off the **Bluggers**, who eventually retreat. The **Warehouse Manager** appears.*
Manager	Well done. You have completed your first quest. Now you must enter this tunnel in order to continue.
	***Sarah** and **Jason** enter the tunnel.*

Scene 3

Sarah and Jason find themselves in a desert.
Sand is blowing all around them.

Sarah	*(Angrily)* I'm boiling.
Jason	*(Getting annoyed)* Stop complaining.
Sarah	What's that figure moving over there?
Jason	*(Surprised)* Oh! It's the Warehouse Manager.
Manager	You have to solve another riddle. What do you get if you cross a kangaroo and a sheep?

Jason	*(Excitedly)* I know this one! My best friend told me at school last week. It's a woolly jumper.
Manager	Correct. Here is what you need for your next quest. Two camels and a jar of rat fleas.
	*The **Warehouse Manager** disappears.*
Sarah	Let's get on the camels, Jason.
Jason	*(Nervously)* I don't know.
	***Sarah** and **Jason** mount the camels apprehensively.*
Sarah	*(Shakily)* Here we go.
Jason	I wonder what we'll meet?
	After a few moments of travelling …
Sarah	What lives in a desert?
Jason	*(Terrified)* Arrr! Rats.
Sarah	*(Screaming)* Help!
Jason	They're everywhere.
Sarah	Where are the fleas?
Jason	Here. I'll let them out.
	***Jason** opens the jar of fleas and lets them escape.*
Sarah	Look, they are devouring the rats' skin!
Jason	Cool!
Sarah	*(Disgusted)* It's sick, but they're killing the rats.
	One by one the rats are destroyed.
Jason	Phew, that was a close one.
	***Jason** and **Sarah** make their way slowly across the desert.*
Sarah	Look, there's a black tunnel over there.
	They dismount their camels quickly and run into the tunnel.

Scene 4

Sarah and Jason walk through the tunnel and appear on what looks like a disused airfield.

Sarah	Where are we?
Jason	I don't care. How do we get out of here?
	The Warehouse Manager appears in a puff of purple smoke.
Manager	You are in the air zone.
Sarah	What must we do to get out of here?
Manager	If you solve this riddle you must then kill the Giant Gleeks.
Jason	What are the Gleeks?
Manager	They are giant stinging hornets.
Sarah	How are we going to kill them?
Manager	With a slingshot.
Jason	What is the riddle then?
Manager	Why did the butter fly?
Sarah	Is it because he saw the milk float?
Manager	You are correct. I hope to see you alive in the next zone.
	The Warehouse Manager gives them the slingshot and disappears. The sky goes black and the Gleeks come racing down towards them. Jason picks up the slingshot and starts firing stones found on the runway at the Gleeks. One by one, they fall down.
Jason	This is tiring.
	Sarah screams as a Gleek stings her lightly. A squawking sound makes Jason look round and there are two giant pelicans.
Jason	Look, Sarah. There are two birds. I think they want to help us. Why don't we get on them and fly away?
Sarah	That's a good idea. Gather up some stones first though. I think we will need them.
Jason	You chuck the stones and I'll fire the slingshot.
	Sarah and Jason mount the birds and they take off up into the sky, firing stones.
Sarah	I'm out of stones.
Jason	And I've only got two stones left.
Sarah	But there are still three Gleeks.
Jason	Take this one and try and hit that Gleek there.
	Sarah hits the Gleek and it dies. Jason shoots at the last two Gleeks. One dies and the other races towards him.

Jason	Direct the Gleek towards that cliff.
Sarah	Why?
Jason	*(Impatiently)* Don't argue, just do it.
Sarah	Okay.

Sarah hares towards the cliff and at the last moment directs the bird over the top. The other bird follows but the Gleek does not swerve quickly enough, hits the cliff, dying.

Scene 5

*Suddenly the **Warehouse Manager** appears in a puff of smoke.*

Manager	Here I am. You must answer this riddle. It's not very tough. What has teeth but doesn't bite?

*The **Warehouse Manager** produces a comb from his pocket and uses it on his hair.*

Sarah	I know the answer. It's a comb. A comb has teeth and doesn't bite.
Manager	Well done. That was the easy task. Now for the hard one. To get to the King of the Orb, you must defeat Garuda. He has the sting of the Gleeks from the air zone. He has fierce jaws and he has the venom spitting ability of the Blugger from the water zone. Oh yes. And he can transform into anything solid. To defeat him, you must send an arrow into his heart.
Sarah	Where do we get a bow and arrow from?
Manager	Me, of course. Here you go.

*The **Warehouse Manager** hands the bow and arrow to **Jason**.*

Manager	See you. Here comes Garuda. I can smell him. I forgot to tell you he has dreadful breath. Remember the heart!

*The **Warehouse Manager** vanishes.*

Garuda	I spy with my little eye, two little children with an arrow.
Sarah	Quick, fire the arrow Jason, fire!

***Jason** does as he is told.*

Jason	I've missed, I've missed!

*The arrow carries on and hits a shelf with a glass bottle on it. The bottle smashes to the floor and in the confusion **Garuda** falls, piercing his heart on the broken shards.*

Jason	*(Excitedly, jumping up and down with **Sarah**)* We've done it, we've done it!

*As **Garuda** lies dying on the floor, he utters his final words …*

Garuda	*(Slowly and quietly)* This will not be the last you see of my world and me.
Sarah	Quick, let's get out of here and find the King of the Orb.
	They search for what seems like hours. A light is seen glowing.
Jason	Look, Sarah, over there. In the corner.
Sarah	It looks like a faint glow.
Jason	Walk towards it.
Sarah	It's him, it's him.
The King	Open this orb that I give you now and all the goodness will return to your world and mine.
	The King *hands the orb to* ***Sarah.***
Sarah	I've dropped it!
	The orb breaks and ***Sarah*** *and* ***Jason*** *return to their home, standing over a board game.*
Jason	Mum, Dad, we're back!
	Jason *and* ***Sarah*** *run downstairs to see their mum and dad sitting at the table with their backs to them.*
Sarah	Have you missed us?
Dad	We didn't know you were missing, did we, Mum?
	On saying these words, ***Mum*** *and* ***Dad*** *turn around. They are skeletons.* ***Sarah*** *and* ***Jason*** *look at each other and scream.*

By Jamie Courtney, aged 10
Matthew Keightley, aged 10
Laurence Hanoman, aged 10
Lucy Brown, aged 10
Dean Barden, aged 10
Harvey Bell, aged 10
Shaun Cassidy, aged 10
Sam Sturtivant, aged 10
Darren Bartlett, aged 10
David Fear, aged 10

Offwell VC CE Primary School, Honiton
South West Winners

Jurassic Monopoly

Main characters

Sarah, Jason, Triceratops, Game Keeper

Jason	*(Uncertain)* Which way, do you think?
Sarah	*(After a slight pause, pointing)* That way!
	They enter a large wide open space with huge dinosaur footprints on it ... and a dice.
Sarah	Where are we?
Jason	We are inside my game of Jurassic Monopoly and we are near the start. There's a long way to go so you have to stay calm. You've got to throw the dice to move through the game. You start.
Sarah	Here goes then.
	Sarah *throws a five and the board moves them on five spaces to a roar card square.*
Jason	This could be good or bad, it depends, let's read what ours says!
Sarah	You are given a weapon, a coconut gun and coconuts to go in it! *Yes*, like that is going to protect us!
Jason	That is all you have in this game and they are very effective, honestly!

The dice appears again.

Jason	We can move on once we roll … there you go, a three. Uh oh!
Sarah	What is it?
Jason	Hunting Ground.
Sarah	I don't like the sound of that. What do we have to do?
Jason	Follow the footprints and hopefully find the treasure.
Sarah	Why hopefully?
Jason	Sometimes you find man-eating dinosaurs and die.
Sarah	That's really great, why couldn't you have been playing a normal game?

Sarah looks up.

Sarah	*(Screams)* AAHH! D-dd-dinosaurs!
Jason	You'll see plenty of them before the game is over, it's the main theme!
Sarah	Quick, start shooting before they eat us!

Jason shoots the dinosaur and it disappears, leaving the dice in its place.

Jason	We must have completed the square. Super, let's get out of here!
Sarah	My thoughts exactly! Good thinking for once!

Jason throws the dice.

Sarah	A two!

The game flashes by as they move two spaces forward to the caves.

Jason	Oh, the caves. I was hoping we wouldn't have to go here, it's one of the hardest parts of the game. You have to release the hostages from the dinosaur lair.

The children creep around the caves and are very quiet and careful not to disturb anything.

Jason	*(Whispering)* Not long now, Sarah.
Sarah	*(Pointing ahead)* What is that?
Jason	That is who we have to rescue, but it must be done silently so as not to wake up the sleeping dinosaur or he will eat us! You are more gentle than me so it will have to be you.
Sarah	Great!

Sarah creeps through the dinosaur's legs and releases the caveman who runs off quickly.

Jason and Sarah have completed another square and see a rope ladder, which they climb. This takes them to the awaiting dice. Sarah throws a three.

Jason	Quick, we've landed on the weapon's maze square which means that we have only got thirty seconds to collect as many fighting weapons as we can.
Sarah	*(Looking around)* Wow ... look at all of these. Let's take a spear, coconut gun and the club.
Jason	Just collect the club and I'll get the rest. There's no time to waste. GO!
	She gets out just in time.
Sarah	*(Panting)* That was close!
Jason	Right. Now, roll the dice, we are nearly half way through but the worst is yet to come!
Sarah	A five! Move on five spaces. Where is that going to take us?
Jason	I think we're safe, it's the herbivore dinosaur compound. They don't eat people, they just eat trees and leaves!
Sarah	That's a relief!
Jason	These dinosaurs talk to you if you ask them questions.
	*A **triceratops** walks towards them.*
Sarah	I still don't trust them. You can do all the talking.
Jason	*(To the dinosaur)* Excuse me, can you help me?
Triceratops	Hello there, little person, what do you want?
Sarah	*(Whispering to Jason)* Are you sure he won't eat us?
Jason	Positive!
Sarah	*(To the dinosaur)* We would really like to move through this square as quickly as we can. Can you take us?
Triceratops	Sure, climb up on my back and we'll be there in no time. You'll find the dice waiting for you when we get there!
	The children hold on and after a bumpy ride over the hills they arrive at the edge of the square.
Sarah	It was lovely meeting you.
Triceratops	The pleasure was all mine! Good luck with Dino and Bobo – you can do it!
	***Jason** picks up the dice and throws a six.*
Jason	A six! That means I can throw again! *(He throws)* A one!
Sarah	By my calculations I believe that we might need those weapons that we collected. This is it!
Jason	Yes. I can see the destruction left by King Dino and Bobo!
	The children look around them and see trees toppled and carcasses of rotting people and herbivores.

Sarah	I'm scared, Jason, do you know what to do?
Jason	I've done this level loads, don't worry. Just listen to my instructions and you'll be all right!
	Jason throws his spear at one of the dinosaurs and misses.
Jason	Don't worry, I've got two more chances! Here goes with the gun!
	He fires the gun and the coconuts hit Bobo. Bobo is so big that he can't get up again.
Jason	One down, one to go. This is the hardest one. Keep your fingers crossed for me, Sarah!
	Jason runs up to King Dino from behind and hits him on the head repeatedly.
Jason	Take that, and that, and that …
	All of a sudden, King Dino gives an almighty roar and disappears.
Sarah	You were really so brave. I have to admit, I didn't think you would make it!
Jason	Me neither! To be honest, I've never completed that level before but at least now I know what to do!
Sarah	I'm glad you didn't tell me that earlier.
	The dice suddenly appears next to them. Sarah throws.
Sarah	It's a three. Where does that take us?
Jason	To a roar card, I think. Yes, here we go.
	The children move to the square and the card appears.
Sarah	What does the card say?
Jason	It's a get out of game free card! A card that will enable us to leave the game when we land on the great escape square.
Sarah	Where's that one?
Jason	We could land on it by throwing a five … if I don't, we'll have to go around the board again!
Sarah	I don't think that I could take that!
	Jason holds the dice in his hands.
Jason	Here goes!
	Jason throws. The dice rolls and rolls and eventually lands on a five. The children breathe a sigh of relief.
Sarah	Well done, Jason, I am so proud of you.
	They move forward five spaces.
Jason	We should see the Jurassic game keeper in this square somewhere and he will take the card from us and release us from the game!

Sarah	Is this him?
	She points to a little old man who comes towards them.
Game Keeper	You got the card then?
Sarah	Here it is!
Game Keeper	Thank you for playing the game. Please come again.
Jason	I don't think we will. Well, not from inside the computer anyway!
	*At that moment, a bright light shines on them and they recognise the sight in front of them. It is **Jason's** bedroom!*
Jason	Hey, we must be on the computer screen! I hope someone comes soon to help us.
	At that moment, their dad walks into the bedroom.
Sarah and Jason	DAD! DAD!
	*The children shout as loudly as they can and **Dad** looks around for them.*
Sarah	We're in here. In the computer!
Jason	OVER HERE, DAD!
	***Dad** sees the children and races over to the computer.*
Sarah and Jason	Print us out, Dad! It's the only way!
	***Dad** fiddles with the computer mouse. The printer starts to print. **Sarah** and **Jason** appear on the printed page, flat.*
Dad	I'll have to prise you off the page and work on making you normal again. How on earth did you get into this mess?
Sarah and Jason	It's a monster of a tale, Dad!

By Catherine Yu, aged 10
Nnenna Ngwa, aged 10
Thomas Myring, aged 10
Jack Harvey, aged 10
Connie Clark, aged 10
Natasha Punia, aged 10
Anup Raja, aged 10

Ratcliffe College Junior Dept, Leicester
East Midlands Winners

LOST in the Game

Main characters
Sarah, Jason, Haddi, Dragon, Umbongo

Jason	*(Uncertain)* Which way, do you think?
Sarah	*(After a slight pause, pointing)* That way!
	*They set off, **Sarah** in the lead. The scene quickly changes to a cabbage field.*
Jason	Hey look! There's a trail of huge cabbages.
Sarah	Let's follow them.
	They walk along the trail until they reach a building.
Jason	There are five doors. Which shall we go through?
Sarah	*(Pointing)* That one. Look, the floor is moving!
Jason	Let's go through that door.
	They go through the door.
Sarah	Watch out, there's a huge eagle!
Jason	Run!
	***Sarah** accidentally steps on a button in the middle of the floor.*
Sarah	Look, there's three jewels flying out.
Jason	Catch them, quick! They might bring us good luck.

The children manage to grab them.

Sarah	Quick! The eagle is going to dive. We'd better get out before it catches us.
Jason	Let's try another door.

They stand on the revolving floor and go through another door to find themselves in a forest.

Sarah	Look, there's two paths. Which shall we take?
Jason	Let's take the rough path. The baddies might want us to take the other one.

Suddenly they hear sad crying.

Sarah	*(Worried)* What's that?
Jason	We'd better go and find out.
Sarah	It's getting louder, we must be nearer.
Jason	It sounds like it's coming from up above us.
Sarah	*(Looking around)* It must be up a tree.
Jason	It is! *(Pointing)* Look in that oak tree over there.
Sarah	Oh look! It's a little monkey.
Monkey	*(With his arms over his head)* Don't take me too. I haven't done anything wrong.
Sarah	What are you talking about? We don't want to hurt you. We want to help you.
Monkey	Phew! You're not spies for the Wolf Men, are you?
Jason	*(Puzzled)* Who are the Wolf Men?
Monkey	They're the monsters who've captured my father, Umbongo, and they're planning to take over the world.
Sarah	Come down here so we can talk to you.

*The **monkey** climbs down cautiously.*

Sarah	What's your name?
Monkey	Haddi. Please help me rescue my father. Have you seen any gems on your travels?
Jason	Yes, I've got them in my pocket.

He reaches into his pocket and pulls out the gems.

Sarah	Are these what you mean?
Haddi	*(Excitedly)* Yes! Yes! Now we can rescue my father.
Sarah	Look! Smoke!
Jason	There's a huge dragon coming out of it!

*The **dragon** approaches.*

Dragon	You are needed to save Umbongo, you're the only ones who can help. Hop on, all of you.

*Sarah, Jason and Haddi all get up onto the **dragon's** back.*

Jason	Where are we going?
Dragon	Maglorosa Mountain.

They take off with a jolt.

Haddi	Whee! Whee! I'm flying.

*After a while, **Sarah** sees something below them.*

Sarah	What's that square thing down there?
Dragon	It's a door in the mountain. That's where Umbongo is. I'll fly down so you can see it.

They fly down and land smoothly.

Dragon	*(With humour)* I had a good flying teacher.
Haddi	*(Bravely, to the rest of them)* You hide behind those big rocks and I'll knock on the door.
Sarah	Are you sure this is safe?
Haddi	Well, it's the only way to get my father back.
Sarah	Okay then.

Haddi knocks firmly on the door. The door creaks open and three hunched figures with glowing eyes, terrifying faces and claw-like fingers appear. They are the Wolf Men.

Sarah	*(From behind the rock, whispering)* Take care, Haddi.

Haddi disappears up the mountain and the Wolf Men scramble after him.

Jason	Quick, let's go through the door and find Umbongo.

*Jason runs forward and **Sarah** and the **dragon** rush after him.*

Jason	Look there's a huge cage in the corner over there and there's somebody in it.
Sarah	He's massive! Doesn't he have the strength to get out of that cage?
Dragon	That's where you come in. Drop the gems into the cage, okay?

Jason pulls the gems out of his pocket and drops them.

Dragon	Now he can get his strength back. He has an earring in one ear, without the gems in it he is powerless so he needs to put them in to regain his powers.

Umbongo puts them in.

Dragon	He can get out of the cage now and save the world from the Wolf Men. Umbongo can kill them easily now that he has his power back.
	Haddi *bursts in, followed by the Wolf Men.*
Jason	Umbongo's ripping open the cage, but hang on, now what's he doing?
Sarah	He's killing the Wolf Men! Hurrah for Umbongo!
	Sarah *throws her hands in the air and cheers.*
Dragon	He only needs to punch a Wolf Man and the Wolf Man is dead.
Haddi	Dad! Dad! You're alive! And we rescued you.
	Haddi *introduces the children to **Umbongo.***
Umbongo	Thank you again, Sarah and Jason. Because you have saved me, and the world, you can each have one wish.
Jason	I wish that we could get home in time for tea.
Umbongo	Your wish shall be granted.
Sarah	I wish we could remember this day for the rest of our lives.
Umbongo	Your wish shall be granted.
Dragon	Well, I'd better be on my way. Bye!
	He flies up into the sky.
	Jason's *wish is granted and the children arrive home in time for tea.*

By Kirsty Roche, aged 9
Mark Taylor, aged 9
Rose Hiles, aged 9
Edward Wise, aged 9
Andrew Taylor, aged 9
Rebecca Veerman, aged 9
Emily Leggott, aged 9

Croft CE School, Darlington
Yorkshire and Humberside Winners

The Journey of the Block

Main characters

Sarah, Jason

Scene 1

Jason	*(Uncertain)* Which way, do you think?
Sarah	*(After a slight pause, pointing)* That way!
	*They set off, **Sarah** in the lead. The scene changes quickly to a dark space with a dim light showing. **Sarah** and **Jason** walk on and look around. The light is a block of colours which suddenly appears. The children walk over to the colour block and stare at it suspiciously. **Sarah** puts her hand in it. The block spins slowly.*
Sarah	*(Really worried)* Help! My hand's stuck!
Jason	Oh yeah. I'm sure. You're just trying to trick me, as usual.
Sarah	Just help me, you idiot.
Jason	What shall I do?
Sarah	Pull my hand out of this coloured thing.
	***Jason** gets hold of her arm and pulls with both hands.*
Jason	I'm trying, I'm trying.

	Sarah's arm begins to move into the block of colours.
Sarah	*(Shouting)* Help, I'm being sucked in! Quick!
	Jason grabs Sarah's legs and they both get sucked into another dimension.

Scene 2

A hut, some trees and water and a dragon in the distance

Jason	Where are we?
Sarah	*(Sarcastically)* How am I supposed to know?
Jason	*(Pointing)* Look over there!
	Sedra floats into view.
Sarah	*(Looking everywhere except the water)* Where?
Jason	Over there, that floating sedra in the water.
Sarah	*(Still looking everywhere except the water)* What are you on about?
Jason	Look, that big blue water dragon. I saw it in a book.
Sarah	*(Screaming)* A dragon! Where?
Jason	On the horizon. We'd better move.
	The children run in the opposite direction from the dragon.
Sarah	*(Cautiously)* This isn't our world, is it?
Jason	There's a small hut. We can hide.
	Sedra is moving towards them.
Sarah	We'd better not waste time. This is all your fault.
	They move towards the hut but then they both fall down a hole. Sarah and Jason scream. Lights go on and the children pick themselves up.

Scene 3

A fairground

Jason	Now where are we?
Sarah	It's a fair! Come on, make the most of it. Let's get some candy floss and go on the big wheel.
	They walk over to the candy floss machine, buy some candy floss and begin to eat it.
Jason	This is good.
Sarah	*(Looking around)* Oh look. There's the big wheel.
	They run towards the wheel and get in an empty seat. The lights go out. Sarah and Jason scream.

Scene 4

A hedge maze

Lights go on.

Jason   We're in a maze.

They are surrounded by new scenery, a maze hedge. They walk around the maze.

Sarah   Let's get out of this place. I don't like it.

Jason   Now who's a wimp? There's a gap in the hedge.

Sarah   Quick then! Hurry up!

They walk through the gap.

Jason   *(Moodily)* It's a dead end.

Sarah   *(In a real bossy way)* You're the one who got us here and you're going to get us out. So there!

Jason   Okay, okay. Sorry. That way then. *(Pointing left)*

Sarah   You'd better be right this time.

Jason   Come on, hurry up.

Sarah   I'm coming, I'm coming.

They run through a gap.

Jason   We're on a roll.

Sarah   Shut up, you idiot.

Jason   *(Screwing up his face)* Stop being so bossy.

Sarah   Are you calling me bossy? You should look in the mirror then.

Jason   Yeah, I am calling you bossy. I'll get out of this place myself then.

***Jason** walks away.*

Sarah   I'll be able to get out by going my own way.

Jason   *(Laughing)* I bet you can't.

Sarah   Just watch me then.

She moves a couple of steps the other way.

Jason   *(Hesitantly)* See you when you get home, if you ever do!

Sarah   I won't even think about it.

***Jason** walks through another gap, so they are either side of a hedge.*

Sarah   *(Quietly)* He never admits he's a dimwit.

Jason   *(To himself)* She thinks she's going to beat me. Huh! I'll show her!

Sarah   It's his fault. He got me into this mess.

Jason	I'll soon be there if I stop thinking about her.
	*The coloured block has appeared again and opened up in front of **Sarah**. She walks towards it.*
Sarah	Look, there's the coloured block. I'm going to beat Jason and show him who knows best.
Jason	*(Seeing the block)* Yes! I'm going to beat her to the block.
	They both arrive at the block at the same time.
Sarah	*(In a disappointed voice)* So.
Jason	Can we go home now?
Sarah	*(Moodily)* I suppose so, if we have to.
Jason	*(Shouting)* YES!
	***Sarah** and **Jason** jump into the block. Curtains close, lights go out. The maze disappears.*

Scene 5

Back home, Sarah's bedroom

Sarah	Well!
	She stands up and tidies her clothes.
Jason	Guess what?
Sarah	*(In a bored voice)* What?
Jason	We're back home.
	***Sarah** and **Jason** look at each other apologetically.*
Sarah	Sorry!
Jason	I don't think we will play that game again.
	They both laugh.

By Clare Edwards, aged 10
Annie Matthews, aged 9

Hampton Dene County Primary School, Hereford
West Midlands Winners

Game Trap

Main characters

Sarah, Jason, Lara Croft, Koga, the King of the Game

Scene 1

Jason	*(Uncertain)* Which way, do you think?
Sarah	*(After a slight pause, pointing)* That way!
	*They set off, **Sarah** in the lead. The scene quickly changes to ...*

Scene 2

The jungle, level one

Sarah	*(Scared)* Where are we?
Jason	I don't know!
Sarah	Oh great. Nothing could get worse!
Jason	Wanna bet? We're sinking in quicksand!
	The sand is up to their knees.
Sarah	This is all your fault!
Jason	I can get us out of this!
Sarah	Oh yeah, how? That's what you said last time!

51

	A snake dangles down.
Jason	There's a rope – grab it!
Sarah	Er, Jason, do ropes hiss?
Snake	Ssssssss!
Jason	Quick – jump off!
Sarah	Phew! That was a close one!
	Sound of a tiger.
Jason	What was that? This place creeps me out, I'm out of here!
	*He makes to run off stage, but **Sarah** stops him.*
Sarah	Don't be such a baby!
	They turn around and there stand six tigers.
Sarah	Let's take the other way.
Jason	I don't think that way is available.
	There are six more tigers. The children are surrounded.
Sarah	I see what you mean!
Jason	Any ideas, Sar?
Sarah	Fire!
Jason	But I haven't got a gun!
Sarah	Not that fire, dumbo! Light a fire!
Jason	*(Frantically)* How?
Sarah	*(Impatiently)* Like this! Pick up two sticks rub them together – see!
	*Eleven tigers run off. One stays behind and lunges at **Jason** but it is scared off by the fire and runs off as well. Voice from nowhere sounds.*
Voice	You have passed level one. Level two is more advanced so I will give you a weapon to help you survive!

Scene 3

The swamp, level two

Sarah	How are we gonna get over this huge puddle, eh?
Jason	I don't think it's a puddle, Sar! *(Looking pleased)* There's a log! Let's climb on and float over. We'll be there in no time!
Sarah	Jason. This 'log' is green!
Jason	*(In a couldn't-care-less voice)* Covered in moss probably.

Sarah	I'll try again. Jason? Do logs have eyes?
Jason	Eyes! Don't be stupid, logs don't have eyes!
Sarah	Then look by your feet. What do you see?
Jason	I see two eyes and a mouth full of sharp teeth. Teeth! I think you're right, Sar! We're standing on a ...
Sarah and Jason	CROCODILE!
Sarah	Quick, I've got an idea. Get your bow and arrow out!
Jason	I don't ...
Sarah	Oh, give it to me. *I'll* use it!
	Sarah shoots.
Sarah	Bullseye!
Jason	Good shot, sis!
	The crocodile sinks to the bottom of the swamp.
Sarah	What now, clever clogs?
Jason	I guess we have to cross that wooden bridge. I'll lead since I'm the oldest!
Sarah	*(Quietly muttering)* And the dumbest!
Jason	What?
Sarah	Nothing. Lead on, lead on!
	Jason is half-way across the bridge when a plank snaps.
Jason	Aaarrrggghhh! Help me, Sarah!
Sarah	Come on, you can make it! Next time keep hold!
	Sarah pulls Jason up.
Jason	At last! We're over.
Sarah	Good. Now I think we'll go that way.
	Sarah points off stage, walks off stage and then back on.
Jason	Hey, Sarah, there's a gun. Grab it!
	A lion comes from behind a bush.
Sarah	I don't think that gun is available!
	Sarah makes a grab for the gun.
Jason	Watch out, sis!
Sarah	It's all right, I've got the gun!
	Sarah shoots, killing the lion.

Jason	Hey, cool. This is an oozy like Tomb Raider!
Sarah	Duh! This *is* Tomb Raider!
Jason	How do you know?
Sarah	'Cos there's Lara Croft!
Lara	Hi! I'm Lara. You have completed level two. Here is a sword and a shield to protect yourselves against Koga!
Jason	Who's Koga?
Sarah	And what's that temple in the distance?
Lara	Koga is the mighty King of the Game and that temple is his home!
Sarah	So what's Koga got to do with us?
Lara	You have to defeat Koga to be released from the game.
Sarah	Oh!
Lara	I've never done it. I'm stuck. I warn you, Koga is a shape shifter and he only gives you three chances to defeat him. I've had them.
Jason	Come on, Lara, Sarah, let's go!
Lara	*(Exasperated)* Haven't you learned anything! I can't defeat Koga any more. I'm an outcast!
Jason	*(Disappointed)* Oh! Well, come on, Sarah. We'll defeat Koga on our own!

Scene 4

Koga's temple, level three

Sarah	*(Awed)* So you're the mighty Koga?
	Koga *has taken the form of a large tiger.*
Koga	Yes! I am Koga.
	Koga *roars.*
Jason	*(Quietly)* Here goes! *(Louder)* We challenge you!
Koga	Ha ha ha! I've never had such a pair of WIMPS!
	Koga's *shape shifts into a six headed bull.*
Jason	Er …
Sarah	Don't be a baby! *(Turning to **Koga**)* We'll do it!
Koga	I accept! The battle begins – NOW!
Sarah	Jump! Get the gun and shoot!
Jason	Right! Yahoo! He's down!
Koga	You've defeated me once. Twice more to go!

Koga changes into a crocodile. Jason shoots him with the bow and arrow.

Jason	Got him again!
Koga	You won't get away with this!
Sarah	I want a go! Give me that sword! Hy-a!

Sarah kills Koga.

Sarah and Jason	We won!

By Kara Pickering, aged 9
Gemma King, aged 9
Philip Douglas, aged 9
Matthew Urwin, aged 9
Mark Paterson, aged 9

Fairfield Junior School, Stockton-on-Tees
North East Winners

Remember, It's Only a Game!

Main characters
Sarah, Jason, Games Master

Scene 1

Jason	*(Uncertain)* Which way, do you think?
Sarah	*(After a slight pause, pointing)* That way!
	*The children argue. **Jason** pushes **Sarah**.*
Sarah	Ow! I'm lying on something. What is it?
Jason	Let me see!
Sarah	It's part of a key!
	Suddenly there is a whirlwind. The children stand rooted to the spot, looking very shocked.
Games Master	Please children do stop now, I do not want you to have a row. You have now entered the Challenge Game, And will need three parts of a key all the same, I'm sure mummy can help you here, But you might get a bit of a shock, my dears, Remember it's only a game!
	The last line is repeated three times, getting quieter each time.

Scene 2

Inside a pyramid

Sarah	Mummies! What on earth is he talking about?
Jason	I've got it! We're in a pyramid, aren't we, there must be mummies somewhere! You know! He means the ancient Egyptian rolls of bandages!
Sarah	Yes, over there! They look strange. I've never seen one before.
Jason	But which one though? There's loads of them! We'll have to look at all of them.

Sarah sits on a colourful tomb.

Jason	*(Panicking)* It's got to be in there! Get up, Sarah, quick!

Jason lifts up the lid of the tomb.

Sarah and Jason	*AARRGGHH!*

Jason drops the lid of the tomb with a crash.

Sarah	*(Quickly, in a frightened voice, pointing at the tomb)* There she is, but look at her head, look at the snakes!
Jason	Never mind the snakes. Look what she's holding, it's part of the key! You get it, Sarah.
Sarah	No way! If you're so brave, you get it! Remember it's only a game.
Games Master	Remember it's only a game, Remember it's only a game, Remember it's only a game.

Jason shuts his eyes and puts his hand in quickly. He grabs the key.

Jason	I've got it! Hooray! We can nearly go home!
Sarah	Great! We've got the second part of the key!
Games Master	Well done, children, you have not failed me yet, Remember you still have one more piece to get, Horoscopes and birthdays will give you a clue, Remember it's only a game, remember it's only a game, Remember it's only a game.
Jason	*(With expression)* What is he talking about, birthdays and horoscopes! Have you got any idea?
Sarah	Don't you get it? We have to see what star signs we are and maybe they will give us a clue.
Jason	Well, my birthday is on the seventeenth of June and I'm a Gemini. Let me think. No, there's no clues about mine. Yours might give us a hint.

Sarah	Let's check my birthday then. Mine's on the twelfth of November and I'm a Scorpio. I can't think of anything to do with Scorpio.
Jason	Er … Sarah. I thought of Scorpions. It might not be, though.
Sarah	NO! It can't be!

Sarah looks at Jason in complete horror.

Jason	*(Uncertain, pointing)* There's a deep pit over there. I wonder if it's got anything to do with this challenge?

They nervously creep over, being very cautious.

Sarah	AARRGGHH! There's scorpions over there! I'm not going anywhere near them. No way! Even if you paid me, I wouldn't!
Jason	They can't hurt you. Remember it's only a game.
Games Master	Remember it's only a game, it's only a game, it's only a game.
Sarah	I'm not going anywhere near them no matter what you say. Scorpions are dangerous and deadly.
Jason	Do you want to get out of this game or not? Just think, you're letting me down here as well. Maybe you're scared of scorpions but I'm not.
Sarah	Oh, okay! There's one condition though, you have to help me out if I fall in or anything.
Jason	That's fine by me.

Sarah reaches down and grabs the sparkly key.

Jason	*(Grinning, joyously)* Great! We have all of the key! We can go home!
Sarah	Well, how do we actually get home? I mean, there's hardly anything to help us. We'll be stuck here for ever, thanks to you!
Games Master	Well done, children, you've passed the test, I think you deserve a well earned rest, Sail the sea, With your key, But hold on tight, The waves may not be slight, When you come to shore, You'll see a door, Remember it's only a game, remember it's only a game, Remember it's only a game.

Scene 3

Outside the pyramid

Jason   Listen! What's that noise? It sounds like water swishing about, like in our bath at home.

Sarah   Don't be silly, Jason. Look! It's over there. There's a lake and some little boats. I suppose the Games Master wants us to sail in these.

They climb in and set sail.

Jason   This is so peaceful. I could fall asleep right now. The water is so gentle and calm.

Sarah   Why do you always talk of going to sleep? Wake up!

Jason   What's that in the distance? It looks like some kind of rapids.

Sarah   *(Very panicky)* What! We can't steer away from them, we're going to drown. We'll have to start shouting.

They both shout as loudly as they can.

Sarah   Shout louder, Jason. We have to have help!

Jason   There's no point. Remember what the Games Master said. After all it's only a game.

Games Master   Remember, it's only a game, remember it's only a game, remember it's only a game.

Jason   Hold on tight, Sarah, these waves are enormous! Prepare for a bumpy ride.

Sarah   I'm soaked through! We're going to get into so much trouble when we get home.

Jason   Look! Here's the shore! We can go home!

Ahead is another pyramid. They find a door in it.

Sarah   Oh no! Not another pyramid!

Jason   There's a keyhole!

He turns the key in the lock. Everything spins round and round.

Scene 4

Back home

Jason   I had a strange dream last night. There was this Games Master and he gave us all kinds of riddles. We had to go in a pyramid and find the mummy that held part of our key. Next, you had to put your hand in a scorpions' pit to grab another part of the key. It was so funny, you squealing!

Sarah   Hey! You're cruel! Did it end with us going on some rapids in a little wooden boat that rocked violently every time a wave hit it?

Jason *(Amazed)* How did you know it ended like that? It's really strange that you should know too.

Sarah I was there, wasn't I? We didn't both have the same dream. It really happened.

In the morning, their mother comes in. She notices they are dirty and wet, and marches them into the bathroom.

By Stephanie Bissell, aged 10
Sophie Moar, aged 10
Danielle Murrell, aged 10

Roke Primary School, Croydon
London Winners

Into the Future

Main characters
Sarah, Jason, Ben, the five Creators, Moon Munchkins

Jason	*(Uncertain)* Which way, do you think?
Sarah	*(After a slight pause)* That way!
	*Suddenly the light flashes on and **Sarah** and **Jason** find themselves being controlled by a person playing a computer game called 'Into the Future'. The person – Sarah and Jason's friend **Ben** – is very puzzled.*
Ben	What's going on? Where are Jason and Sarah? *(Surprised)* Funny, those two on the screen look kind of familiar!
	***Sarah** and **Jason** start to move about like robots.*
Sarah	*(Surprised and scared)* Hang on! I'm moving! But I'm not controlling myself!
Jason	Same here! This is *really* weird!
Sarah	*(Frightened)* Well, there's no time to think about that. *(Pointing)* I think I can see an octopus – a *giant* one!
Jason	Oh, didn't I tell you? This is Jaws, he eats humans for fun! I've been killed on this level *loads* of times.
Sarah	*(Sarcastically)* Oh great! Okay, genius, if you're so smart, how are we going to get past it?
Jason	Well, there is one way, but it means we'll have to get sucked down a whirlpool!
Sarah	*(Even more sarcastically)* Oh, this just gets better and better … Ahhhhh!

	Sarah and *Jason* get sucked down the whirlpool and find themselves in a stage they must complete to get to the next level.
Sarah	Well, here we are in the middle of nowhere. Nobody in sight.
Jason	I wouldn't necessarily say that! We're surrounded by robots!
Creators	*(Speaking with mechanical voices)* Human located! Now exterminate! Human located! Now exterminate!
	Sarah and *Jason* look scared. Suddenly two **men** pop out of two of the robots.
Creators	*(Laughing)* Ha! Fooled you! We were the robots! But we need your help. We can't get out! We were sucked into the game just like you were!
Jason	Who are *you*?
Creators	We are the creators of this game. We got sucked in by accident, while we were making the game!
Jason	Oh, right! I think I know how to get out of here. You have to say 'To Infinity and Beyond' ... woah!
	There is a blinding flash of light and suddenly everyone is in the space level. They are in a hole; around them are stars, the moon and planets.
Sarah	Okay. Where are we?
Jason	We're in the space level. The next level is the end! Whoever's playing it is doing pretty well. You know Sarah, I think it could be Ben. He is the only one who's as good as me *and* he said he was coming round this afternoon.
Sarah	Well, that's some good news. But I'm afraid I've got some bad news. I think we're stuck down a black hole.
Creators	Yes, yes, I think she's right. I'm sure we put a black hole in the space level.
	*Another **creator** enters and crouches down in the corner.*
Creator 3	*(Whispering cautiously)* Hello! Hello! Hello! Is anybody there? Can you hear me?
Jason	Who on earth's that?
Creator 3	Freddie? George? Is that you?
Creators 1 and 2	Johnnie! It's you! *(Turning to **Jason** and **Sarah**)* He's one of us. One of the creators.
	Jason and *Sarah* look around and see *Johnnie* crouching in the corner.
Jason and Sarah	Oh, right!

Jason	Here are the words to get out! You say 'Up and Out!'
All	Up and Out!
	All the characters shoot out of the black hole and find themselves on the moon.
Freddie	I think I know where we are! We put the moon in the space level, didn't we?
George	*(Scratching his head)* Er … to be honest with you, I really can't remember!
Johnnie	Yes, yes, yes, don't you remember? Of course we did!
Jason	You should know, you're a creator! I've been on the moon in this level *plenty* of times!
Sarah	Okay, okay, we get your point. Now what are we supposed to do?
Jason	*(Slowly with his hand to his ear)* Sarah? Sarah, can you hear something?
Sarah	*(Surprised)* Funny you should say that. In actual fact, I *can* hear a strange noise!
Johnnie	Oh no, this means trouble! It's the moon munchkins!
Jason	*(Covering his eyes with his hands)* Oh no, I forgot about them!
	*Suddenly there is a huge banging sound and the **moon munchkins** appear.*
Moon Munchkins	Moon Munchkins! Moon Munchkins!
Johnnie	Grab your laser guns! We have to kill them all to get to the next level!
Sarah	*(Sarcastically)* Oh, great!
	*No one speaks as they concentrate on winning the battle and getting down to earth. There are sounds of gun shots, then **Sarah**, **Jason** and the **three creators** jump up and punch the air as they win the battle. A spaceship appears and everyone gets in it.*
Tommy (Creator 4)	George? Johnnie? Freddie? Is that you? I haven't seen you since we got sucked in! I've been trapped driving this spaceship all this time. I thought you'd never find me!
George	Is that you, Tommy? Well, we wouldn't have got here if it hadn't been for Jason and Sarah.
Tommy	Who are they?
Freddie	*(Pointing at **Jason** and **Sarah**)* Here they are!
Tommy	*(Waving)* Oh. Hi, you two!
Jason and Sarah	Hi!

George	Jason and Sarah rescued us. They got sucked in too, just like we did.
Tommy	How are you going to help *me* get out of here?
Jason	Well, we're going to have to get down to earth first.
	*The spaceship shoots down to earth. They all get out and find themselves in the next level – the rainforest. Around them are trees and all sorts of jungle animals. **Jason** and **Sarah** drag **Tommy** out of the spaceship before he gets trapped in again.*
Tommy	Oh, I know where we are. We are in the rainforest level, which is the last level.
Freddie	Unlucky for us, it's also the hardest level.
George	And we still have to find Jamie, the last creator.
Sarah	*(Sighing with relief)* Oh great, we're finally near the end.
	***Jamie**, creator five, comes running in dressed as a cheetah.*
Johnnie	*(Screaming)* Uh oh, there's a cheetah coming for us!
Jamie	STOP! STOP! I'm not really a cheetah, I'm Jamie the creator. I was trying to catch you up.
George	*(Surprised)* Oh, it's you, Jamie!
Freddie	We were worried we were going to be eaten alive!
Jamie	*(Starting to run)* I think we are, here comes another cheetah!
Sarah	It's probably just another creator, no need to worry.
Freddie	*(Alarmed)* There isn't another creator! RUN!
	They all start to run, scared.
Jason	How can we lose him?
Johnnie	I know, there's a lake further on, we had better head for that.
	They all arrive at the lake and stop, panting.
Sarah	*(Out of breath)* We're here *(Panting)* at last.
Jason	The cheetah is still right behind us.
Freddie	Didn't we put a couple of alligators in this lake?
Johnnie	*(Casually)* Oh yeah, we did put in about twelve, didn't we?
Sarah	Oh no, I wish you hadn't put so many dangerous creatures in the game!
	Alligators' noses pop up from the water.
Jason	I know, let's jump on their noses and run across.
Sarah	*(Looking scared)* What if they bite me, though?
Jason	Don't be so wet. Get it – wet?

Sarah	*(Sarcastically)* Oh ha ha, very funny.
Jason	Let's go!
	Everyone jumps across, using the alligators as stepping stones.
Freddie	*(Gasping for breath)* We're across, we're actually across!
Sarah	I'm *never* going near an alligator *ever* again!
	A bright archway appears at one end of the stage.
Jason	*(Pointing and looking happy)* Sarah, Sarah! Look at that shining archway! Do you think it could be our way home?
Sarah	*(Smiling)* Wow, Jason, I think you might be right! Let's try going through it!
Creators	Yes, let's!
	*Everyone walks through the archway, **Sarah** and **Jason** leading the way.*
Sarah and Jason	Here we go, we're being sucked OUT!
Everyone	Aaaggghhh!
	*Everyone climbs out of the computer screen, in Jason's bedroom. **Ben** is sitting at the desk. There is a bed in the room and a table with some books on it.*
Jason	Phew! I can finally feel my feet on solid ground again!
Sarah	Thank heaven for that!
	***Ben** turns around and gasps.*
Ben	Jason, Sarah, it's you! Where have you been?
	*The **creators** exit by the window. **Sarah, Jason** and **Ben** go downstairs for tea.*
Mum	I saw five strange men walking down the road just now. Do you know who they are?
Sarah	*(Hesitating)* Well … sort of.
Mum	*(Surprised) I* didn't recognise them! Who are they! How do you know them?
Jason	It's a long story!

By Laura Thomas, aged 10
Helen Bamber, aged 10
Bethany Rankine, aged 10

Mossley CE Primary School, Congleton
North West Winners

The Murder of Doctor Black

Main characters

Sarah, Jason and 'Cluedo' characters

Scene 1

Jason	*(Uncertain)* Which way, do you think?
Sarah	*(After a slight pause, pointing)* That way!
	*They set off, **Sarah** in the lead. The scene quickly changes to ...*

Scene 2

The kitchen

Sarah	We're in the kitchen! The kitchen in the game Cluedo!
Jason	Well, we're not exactly in the ballroom, are we?
Sarah	Shh! I hear footsteps!
	*The footsteps get louder. **Mrs White** bursts in armed with a rolling pin.*
Mrs White	THERE'S BEEN A MURDER! Help! Police! Hello! How did you get in here?
Jason	*(Awkwardly)* We ... er ... don't exactly know. You see ...
Mrs White	What do you mean, you don't know! Next you'll be telling me you got into the secret passage!

Sarah	Well, we did actually!
Mrs White	So you came from the underground to this house?
Jason	No, we …
Mrs White	I don't want to hear it! Out!

She pushes them down the steps of the passage. **Sarah** *stumbles and falls.*

Scene 3

The study

Jason *and* **Sarah** *open the door to the study to find a body that has been strangled to death. The body is of a middle-aged man with a smart suit and greying hair. He is on the floor in what looks like an uncomfortable position. The fire in the study is blazing wildly and the ink from his pen is dripping on the rug.*

Jason	Wow! Some story *I'm* going to tell at school!
Sarah	That's not the point.
Jason	I know it's not. What is the point then?
Sarah	The point is, that if we don't solve this murder mystery we won't be able to go back home. *(Her voice gets louder and sterner)* And I mean it this time, so be as crafty in the game as you are in real life!
Jason	Okay! Okay! Now how about we get started by telling some people about this murder!

They leave to find **Miss Scarlett** *and* **Mrs Peacock** *in the conservatory.*

Scene 4

In the conservatory

They meet **Miss Scarlett** *and* **Mrs Peacock***.*

| **Jason** | *(Sarcastically)* Help! Help! There's been a murder! |

Jason *receives a kick from* **Sarah***. The two women look up from their books and stare for a moment at the children.* **Mrs Peacock** *looks very shocked at the mere sight of scruffy children in the house and* **Miss Scarlett** *has no expression on her face at all. The room itself is filled with exotic plants from Australia to Morocco.*

| **Mrs Peacock** | *(Yawning)* Really? |
| **Miss Scarlett** | Oh? |

Sarah	Yes! A middle-aged man has been strangled to death!
Mrs Peacock	Oh! That'll be Dr Black. *(Under her breath)* Glad someone's got rid of him.
Miss Scarlett	*(Giving **Mrs Peacock** a look)* Let's go and have a look!
Jason	We'll go and find the others.

Scene 5

The billiard room

*Jason and Sarah follow some more passages to the billiard room where they find three drunken men. Sarah and Jason recognise them immediately. They are **Colonel Mustard, Professor Plum** and **Reverend Green**. Each has a glass of whisky in his hands and empty bottles have been thrown around the room. Sarah looks a bit hesitant.*

Sarah	*(Whispering)* I don't like this. Let's go.
Jason	No. Trust me. *(He strolls over to them)* Hey ... er ... there's been a ... erm ... vending machine ... er ... installed in the study. Do you want to look ... perhaps?
	*He strolls back to an annoyed **Sarah**.*
Sarah	Even I could do better than that.
Jason	So?
Sarah	So ... if they don't come we'll never get out of here!
	***Professor Plum** comes over.*
Prof. Plum	Can we come?
	*Jason smirks at **Sarah**.*

Scene 6

The study

***Colonel Mustard, Reverend Green** and **Professor Plum** are a bit disappointed to find a dead body instead of a vending machine. The drunkest of them all, **Professor Plum**, takes it the worst.*

Prof. Plum	*(Wagging a finger at **Jason**)* You told us there was a vending machine here!
Jason	*(Sheepishly)* Erm ... we ... er ... tricked you ... because we wanted to show you this.
	He points at the body.
Prof. Plum	I don't care whether the world is in trouble and only I can save it! You get me my vending machine, otherwise you will be dead with him!

He storms out of the room.

Rev. Green   Wow. Sorry about that.

*A large shadow looms over them and a giant hand reaches in to pick up **Reverend Green**. **Jason** and **Sarah** look up to find that the **real Jason** and **Sarah** are actually playing the game.*

Sarah   *(Waving madly)* Hello! Down *here!*

***Jason** climbs on top of **Reverend Green's** head so that the **real Jason** can see them.*

Jason   *(Trying to keep his balance)* OI! DOWN HERE! HELLO? EARTH TO JASON AND SARAH!

Jason 2   Cool! Little people that look like us!

*He reaches down to pick up **Jason** and **Sarah**. **Jason** squirms in **Jason 2's** palm.*

Sarah 2   Where did they come from?

Jason 2   Dunno. What shall we do with them?

Sarah 2   Leave them. They'll wander off.

***Jason 2** puts **Jason** and **Sarah** down in the kitchen.*

Scene 7

The kitchen

***Jason** and **Sarah** find **Mrs White** with a dead body at her feet and a revolver in her bloodstained hands.*

Mrs White   It's not what you think …

Jason   *(Craftily)* Oh I think we know all right! Go on! Spill the beans!

Mrs White   It wasn't me!

Jason   If it wasn't you, then who was it?

Mrs White   Erm … *(Loudly)* It was Miss Scarlett!

Sarah   Are you sure?

Mrs White   'Course I'm sure. Ask her.

*The door bursts open and **Miss Scarlett** jumps into the middle of the scene.*

Miss Scarlett   Okay, Mrs White! Would you like to say your final prayers?

She pulls out a dagger.

Mrs White   EVERYBODY! MISS SCARLETT DID IT!

Colonel Mustard enters with several men dressed in Army clothes. They scramble around, grab Miss Scarlett and carry her out.

Sarah   Sorry. We just want to go home.

Mrs White   *(Pointing)* Look! The trap door! It's glowing!

Jason   We have to go. Goodbye.

They climb down into the passage.

Scene 8

The passage

Sarah   Well! That was an adventure!

Jason   Yeah! *(Pausing)* What do you think would happen if we went that way?

Jason points to a tunnel with a sign saying:

BEWARE!

ENTER IF YOU DARE!

WELCOME TO MONOPOLY LAND

By Amy Linnell, aged 10
Clare Rowland, aged 10

Stifford Primary School, Grays
East of England Winners

Hagem*

Main characters
Sarah, Jason, Jack, Penny

Jason	*(Uncertain)* Which way, do you think?
Sarah	*(After a slight pause, pointing)* That way!
	They set off, **Sarah** *in the lead. The scene quickly changes to a vast shopping centre where there are small silver game pieces whizzing around the floor on little tracks. It is a giant 3D game board for the game Hagem, a modern (and more sinister) shopping version of 'Monopoly'.*
Sarah	Oh no. What a nightmare! This game has always frustrated me, and here I am inside it. Just great!
Jason	Wow! This is incredible! Look at it, Sarah!
Sarah	Shops, shops, and more shops. Me with no money, and nothing useful in the shops anyway!
Jason	Nothing useful? Haven't you ever bought any of the stuff in these places? I can't believe our luck!
Sarah	So what are we supposed to do now?
Jason	We could go to the bank and get some money.
Sarah	And then what? We can't just stay here! What's the point of this game anyway, 'expert'?
Jason	Well, you have to land on shops, and then you own them and buy and sell stock.
Sarah	And? What is the point?

Jason	You have to make your shop survive the threat of the 'shoplifters'.
Sarah	Shoplifters? What, do they steal your things?
Jason	That's not all they do – they start to eat bits of you.
Sarah	What?! Right, well, that's it! There's no way I'm playing this game.
Jason	Well, surely we'll have to play the game if we ever want to get out of here?
Sarah	I don't know, Jason. It might not be safe.
Jason	You sound like Mum! *(Pauses)* I suppose the teeth trolleys are going to be a bit scary!
Sarah	Is there anything else scary you'd like to tell me about?
Jason	It's probably best if you don't know.
Sarah	Just tell me!
Jason	There are different threats on different levels. For example, if you own Juisters, you have to watch out for cribbles, and if you own Virinico there's the gaps.
Sarah	Gaps?
Jason	They leave gaps in your brain so you can't think straight, and you go crazy, and your shop has to close down. I told you you didn't need to know!
Sarah	Oh! Why did we have to come?

Sarah sits down, her head on her knees. Suddenly, an enormous dice falls down into the centre of one of the open malls, lights flash, and a deafening siren causes Sarah and Jason to cover their ears and screw their eyes up tightly. Their eyes eventually open as they find themselves shooting off along the game piece tracks in different directions.

Sarah	JASON! Where are you going? Please come back!
Jason	Don't worry. Someone's playing the game, and we're obviously the pieces. I'll try to get back to you...ou...ou!

They disappear at speed. Jason eventually stops in a shop called Bangers. The scene is very bright, and there are fireworks fizzing across the ceiling.

Jason	Phew! At least I recognise this place. I've bought this shop before. Can't remember if there were any threats ... *(Pausing to listen to an eerie whining sound)* Who's there? Is somebody there?

Jason walks carefully over to a moving escalator and he notices a small quivering object tucked under the sidepanel. It is a small boy.

Jason	Hello? Who are you? Where did you come from?
Boy	Don't come any closer! I'm not afraid of you!
Jason	There's no reason to be afraid of me. What are you doing here?
Boy	What are you?
Jason	I'm not a 'what', I'm a 'who'. My name's Jason. I'm here with my sister.
Boy	You've got a sister?
Jason	Yes, her name's Sarah – I've just lost her.
Boy	Oh no, oh no, not again!
Jason	What do you mean?
Boy	I came here with my sister. I haven't seen her for years.
Jason	Years?
Boy	We somehow arrived here three or four years ago. I've been looking for her ever since. We can only return together.
Jason	You must be mistaken. You can't have been here that long. What have you been eating?
Boy	Don't need to eat. Time just goes by, but I've stayed the same age.
Jason	Really? What age is that?
Boy	Eight.
Jason	What about your sister?
Boy	She's eight too – we're twins.
Jason	What did you mean about leaving together?
Boy	It was on the orange card. I drew an orange card, and it said: 'You've bought the shop, you've got the stock, leave together or be here forever.'
Jason	You'd better tell me your name.
Boy	I ... I ... can't remember.
Jason	Are there other things you can't remember?
Boy	Is that supposed to be funny?
Jason	No, I mean, do you remember your parents, your house? Things like that.
Boy	Sometimes I have flashes.
Jason	You poor kid. I'll see what I can do to help you.

*The scene changes to a colourful sweetshop, where **Sarah** has landed on a marshmallow couch.*

Sarah	Now what? What on earth is this? Eukk! I hate marshmallow! Jason! Jason! JASON! Can you hear me? *(She struggles out of the couch and looks at the back to front lettering on the shop window: 'Candies')* Candies.
Candies	Who's there?
Sarah	Who's that?
Candies	Are you real?
Sarah	Of course I'm real. Please show yourself. Are you friendly?
Candies	Are *you* friendly?
Sarah	Yes, I'm friendly, where are you?
Candies	You sound a bit like a shoplifter.
Sarah	Well, thanks a bunch! Shoplifter indeed! I've never ever stolen anything in my life!
Candies	They all say that.
Sarah	Oh come on, let's see you.
	A small girl sidles out from behind some giant jars of humbugs.
Sarah	Who are you? What are you doing here?
Candies	You know who I am. You were calling me.
Sarah	Was I?
Candies	Yes. I'm Candies.
Sarah	But that's the name of the shop!
Candies	It's the only name I know.
Sarah	What are you doing here?
Candies	I've got a brother – we're twins. He left me here, and I'm waiting for him.
Sarah	How long has he been gone?
Candies	Long time.
Sarah	Two hours?
Candies	Much longer. Years.
Sarah	Years? You must be confused.
Candies	No, it's true, please believe me. I'm waiting for him. He'll come. The cribbles couldn't get him.
Sarah	Have you seen a cribble?
Candies	Lots, but they can't come in here.
Sarah	Well, it just so happens that I've lost my brother too, so why don't we go out and look for them together?

Candies	Can't go out. He said not to leave.
Sarah	I'm here now – we'll find them. Don't worry.

*Finally, **Sarah** persuades **Candies** to leave the shop and they step onto the tracks in the main mall. At once they are rushed along and deposited roughly in a gloomy shop called 'Griffits'. There is a sound of someone whistling.*

Sarah	I don't like the look of this place.
Candies	I can hear my brother!
Sarah	Can you? Really? Are you sure?
Candies	Can't you hear him?
Sarah	Do you mean that whistling sound?
Candies	My brother can whistle.
Sarah	Look, I don't think it's him. I don't like this shop. I'm taking you back onto the tracks.

They speed off again, and hurtle into a large gardening shop called 'Leafworld'.

Sarah	Well, this is a bit nicer.
Candies	My brother is louder now!
Sarah	I don't mean to be rude, but I think you are imagining that you can hear him.
Candies	No, it *is* him.
Sarah	What's his name?
Candies	J ... Ja ... I'm not sure. I think it's Ja ... something.
Sarah	Jack?
Candies	Yes, that might be it.
Sarah	You are confused, aren't you! JACK! JACK!

*Scene goes back to 'Bangers' where the **boy** is whistling a tune he remembers for **Jason**.*

Jason	I'm sorry, it's not familiar. Maybe you *have* been here a long time! Wait! What's that? Someone's shouting. What are they saying?
Boy	Sounds like my sister.
Jason	Jack! It's Jack they're saying. Is that you, do you think?
Boy	Don't know. Doesn't sound familiar.
Jason	Hello! Sarah? Is that you?
Sarah	*(Calls from off stage)* Jason! Are you all right? I've found a little girl. She needs our help. Maybe that's why we're here.
Jason	Oh Sarah, I'm so glad it's you. Where are you?

Sarah	'Leafworld'. Where are you?
Jason	'Bangers'.
Sarah	I can see you! I can see you! Can you get out of the shop?
Jason	I'll try …
Sarah	Try to keep off the tracks. I'll try to get to you. I'm bringing Candies.
Jason	Why are you bringing candies? I'm not hungry.
Sarah	Stay there, you'll see.

Sarah and Candies manage to clamber over the tracks without being caught up in the speeding jet flows. As they approach 'Bangers', again there is a rumble and screech as the dice is rolled. Sarah and Candies jump into the shop doorway, and Jason pulls open the door.

Jason	I think we've got a matching pair. That's a free ticket out of here!

There is a huge rushing of wind and the four children find themselves swooping upwards. Jason and Sarah find themselves back in their own home, their mother shouting for them to come to dinner. On the TV a voice is speaking excitedly.

Announcer	It's wonderful news for one family this evening. Two eight-year-old twins, Jack and Penny Halliday, who have been missing for twenty-four hours have been found safe and sound in a local shop, 'Candies', the sweet shop in the Hagem Shopping Centre. At the moment they seem to be very confused, but they are both fit and well.

By Aron Journet, aged 9
Gemma Turner, aged 9
Hannah Gunning, aged 9
Marc Godfrey, aged 9

Sutton At Hone CE Primary School, Dartford
South East Winners
*National Winner

poem

A stranger called this morning
Dressed all in black and grey
Put every colour in a bag
And carried them away

The tongue-tingling red of the strawberry ice lolly ...

Roger McGough's lines were inspired by pupils of St Oswald's Worleston C of E Primary School, Nantwich, Cheshire, who sent him some poems, similar in theme to this, which they produced in the course of the Literacy Hour.

INTRODUCING THE POEMS

In Roger McGough's opener, a powerful magician-like thief robs the world of its precious colours – an intriguing subject for a story-poem. In Alexandra's poem, this amazingly daring mega-thief throws the vital colours of the sun, the sea, the sky and the 'green of the crystal grass' into his 'dismal bag'. But what then? That was the challenge for our poets.

Matthew, in his poem, gets mythical: in return for the colours of the earth, the voice in his poem makes a chilling pact with the Devil (for who else is the thief?). Amy, too, sees the thief as a sinister figure 'with a swish of his long black coat', but she feels he can relent and respond to appeals; for her he is mainly an attention-seeker. Aaron's colourful poem ends on a bleak note: 'He ... Left us only darkness / Life will never be the same.' Louise, however, wonders why the thief wants the earth's colours in the first place; she sees him as a sort of cosmic interior-decorator, blazing his huge cave with what he has stolen.

In Otis's poem, the stranger looks at the effects of his thieving: 'Mists of dark and gloomy shadows, / The world was truly VILE!' He is so appalled at what he has done, he undoes the damage himself, without prompting!

But does he have to be flawed or sinister? Not at all, says Claire. In her poem, she has him dressing up in the stolen colours, to become a dazzling Mr Rainbow with a bright lime shirt and blueberry pants. Looked at this way, how can one resist him?

Other poets concentrate less on the figure of the thief, more on what he stole and how it changed the world for them. Christopher lists some beautifully evoked personal images: 'The purple on my relative's / Bright sarong.' and 'The brown of the wood / From my grandad's lathe.' Lee-Anne's poem is a kaleidoscope of things she would sorely miss, from the intimate – 'The battered brown fluff of the much hugged bear' – to the colours of the countryside; she curses 'that wretched man' who leaves them to 'live life in monochrome'. Natalie (in love with rhythm and alliteration) conjures things we all share: 'The smooth, silky silver of the swirling, strolling stars ... The gleaming, gorgeous green of the beautiful jade stone.' Akbar has some arresting images:

The eye melting green of the jealous monster
Dragging itself
Leaving mucus around the lime country.

Did Roger McGough ever finish this poem himself? If so, what did he make of the monochrome stranger? But, maybe, with such competition, he did not feel he needed to – or he didn't dare!

Colourless**

A stranger called this morning
Dressed all in black and grey,
Put every colour in a bag
And carried them away.

The tongue-tingling red of the strawberry ice lolly,
The lifetime of trees evergreen,
The chameleon blue of the ocean,
What's life if they cannot be seen?

What's life without colours to warm us,
A life that is cheerless and sad,
No colours of seasons when changing
Is life you won't wish you had had.

The flowers and shrubs in the garden
Have died in the ground where they stand,
No sunshine had they to feed them,
Nor anything else in this land.

I search in my memory for colours
But find these are missing as well,
Then reach out my mind to locate him,
I find myself hiding in Hell.

I met that stranger this evening,
He laughed with hysterical mirth,
I got the colours back from him,
And scattered them in the earth.

The colours are slowly returning,
Time, it will take them to heal,
But never again will they vanish,
For the Devil and I have a deal.

By Matthew Hughes, aged 10
All Cannings CE Primary School, Devizes
South West Winner
**National Runner-up

Mystery Man

A stranger called this morning
Dressed all in black and grey
Put every colour in a bag
And carried them away

The tongue-tingling red of the
Strawberry ice lolly
Was made into a hat
And even a brolly

It was as tasty as the orange
But not as juicy
Made into a jacket
It looked very fruity

The yellow scrumptious melon
Firm in the hand
When turned into a waistcoat
Looked rather grand

When he turned the green
Into his bright lime shirt
It looked rather sour
But it didn't hurt

The blue as blue as blueberries
Was made into his pants
He jumped around
Like they were full of ants

The indigo was like a plum
Just like the night sky
Was made into his socks
Which made him want to fly

When we added violet shoes
The stranger started to glow
He was no longer dull
He was Mr Rainbow

By Claire Fittes, aged 9
King Edward Primary School, North
Shields
North East Winner

80

A Stranger Called This Morning

A stranger called this morning
Dressed all in black and grey
Put every colour in a bag
And carried them away

The tongue-tingling red of the
strawberry ice lolly
Dazzling light of the orange
All colour gulped away

Off the weird stranger crept
To a cave far away
In a room he hid the colours
Where everything was grey

Noon approached, he stole again
More colours, which he took
Then threw around the cave, for
  once
His life was bright and good!

Apple-green covers the floor,
Plum-blue bounces on the wall
Purple and yellow everywhere
No black and white at all

The cave glowed as if on fire
But then the people came
And all they could do was admire
Colours streaming like the rain!

The people took the colours
The stranger with them flew
And gave him colours to brighten
Himself and others too

The stranger still wants colours
But does not steal them now
His life is brighter now, he is
Innocent, free of sin.

By Louise Turner, aged 10
Hamstreet Primary School, Ashford
South East Winner

The Colour Thief

A stranger called this morning
Dressed all in black and grey
Put every colour in a bag
And carried them away.

The tongue-tingling red of the
  strawberry ice lolly
The slow swaying green of the
  grass
The bright blazing yellow of the
  hot summer sun
The sparkling silver of stars.

He glanced at me quite sternly
His bushy eyebrows raised
His lengthy nose sniffed round for
  more
His cold eyes looked both ways.

The soft fluffy pink of the squidgy
  marshmallow
The clear, cloudless blue of the sky
The crisp crunchy brown of the
  mid-autumn leaves
The bleak white of snowflakes
  that fly.

He left the room quite quickly
With a swish of his long black coat
He touched his hat with a nod
  of his head
All of this brought a lump to
  my throat.

"Please don't take all our colours
  away
Our world will be awfully bland"
He paused and turned whilst
  gritting his teeth
And clenching his gnarled old
  hands.

He smiled and wearily sighed
Whilst putting down his sack
He untied the string from the top
Each colour flooded back!

"I am sorry I've caused you this
  sorrow and pain
But your colours you should
  treasure
So never at any time take them for
  granted
Or I'll take them away at my
  leisure!"

By Amy Walker, aged 10
Kettering Park Junior School, Kettering
East Midlands Winner

82

A Rainbow of Colours

A stranger called this morning
Dressed all in black and grey,
Put every colour in a bag
And carried them away.

The tongue tingling red of the strawberry ice lolly,
The deep, luscious yellow of the gently swaying tulip,
The smooth, silky silver of the swirling, strolling stars,
The calm, peaceful gold of the hot, rising sun,
The deep, delicious purple of the tasty blackcurrant jam,
The gleaming, gorgeous green of the beautiful jade stone.

The world was black and dreary,
All I could do was stare.
I shouted to my neighbours,
"It's that stranger, over there!

Where has he put our colours?
He's taken them away.
Perhaps if we ask him,
He'll bring them back one day.

We bowed our heads and bent our knees
And we began to pray.
"Please bring back our colours.
We'll protect our world always."

By Natalie Chadwick, aged 9
St James (Daisy Hill) CE School, Bolton
North West Winner

Black and White

A stranger called this morning
Dressed all in black and grey
Put every colour in a bag
And carried them away

The tongue-tingling red of the
　　strawberry ice lolly
Will forever be no more
Sitting lonely in the bag
The world is sad and poor

The gorgeous greens in the fields
　　and meadows
Sit miserably with the red
Now our beauty cannot be seen
We might as well be dead!

The blazing yellow of the
　　golden sun
Has been captured by the stranger
Now there is no day and night
We're forever placed in danger

The stranger's bag is heavy
　　with guilt
He has realised what he's done
Looking all around the world
The sadness has just begun

He placed the bag upon his bed
And sat and thought for a while
Mists of dark and gloomy shadows
The world was truly VILE!

No birds were singing in the sky
Which was a sort of grey
It was a sad and expensive price
The stranger had to pay

He let the captured colours go
To their good and rightful place
People know the importance now
Of the colours of the human race!

By Otis Clarke, aged 10
　　Rhodes Avenue Primary School,
　　　Haringey
London Winner

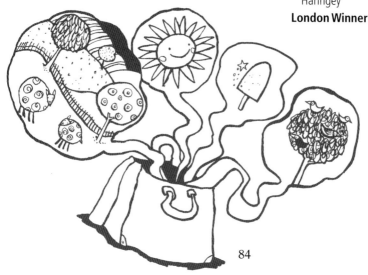

84

Roger McGough's The Sound Collector Adapted for Colour*

A stranger called this morning
Dressed all in black and grey,
Put every colour in a bag,
And carried them away.

The tongue-tingling red of the
strawberry ice lolly,
The glorious gorgeous gold of the
midday sun,
The icy-blue frost of a winter's
morning,
The fluffy grey rabbit sitting in
her run.

My sleeping ginger kitten like a
tiger coiled,
The battered brown fluff of the
much hugged bear,
The ready now ripeness of the
yellow wheat,
The yummy green grapes that I
love to share.

The nutty brown acorns that sit in
the wood,
The beaming sunshine faces of a
field of flowers,
The bright silver lightning that
announces the thunder,
And the crystal like rain of soft
April showers.

The red and yellow flames that
crackle in the hearth,
The beautiful green fields that
stretch on for miles,
The sticky golden syrup that's on
my suet pud,
My mummy's rosy lipstick that
brightens up her smiles.

He's taken all the colours now,
No colours anywhere,
But worst of all, I tell no lie,
The rainbow is now bare.

Curse that wretched man,
Who has finally gone home,
Leaving man upon this earth,
To live life in monochrome.

Curse that wretched man,
Dressed all in black and grey,
Who put every colour in a bag,
And carried them away.

By Lee-Anne Pawley, aged 10
St Mary's CE Primary School,
Southend-on-Sea
East of England Winner
* National Winner

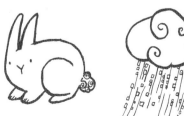

A Stranger Called

A stranger called this morning
Dressed all in black and grey
Put every colour in a bag
And carried them away.

The tongue-tingling red
Of the strawberry ice lolly,
The psychedelic spinning
Of mom's multi-coloured brolly.

The blue of the stunt pegs
On my BMX
The green from the interesting writing
On teletext.

The eternal orange of the sun
Shining all day long.
The purple on my relative's
Bright sarong.

The pink on my face
Before I sunbathe
The brown of the wood
From my grandad's lathe.

The colours of life unimaginable cost
If they were taken, the world would be lost.

By Christopher Javens, aged 10
Willows Primary School, Lichfield
West Midlands Winner

The Colour Thief

A stranger called this morning
Dressed all in black and grey
Put every colour in a bag
And carried them away.

The tongue-tingling red
Of the strawberry ice lolly
Darted into the dark bag
At the touch of his hand.

The yellow of the sun's rays
That sparkles all over the world
Dragged into the dingy bag in one
Swift move.

The shimmering turquoise
Of the pounding sea
Crashed into the dirty black bag
In one almighty movement.

The orange glow of the glamorous
    setting sun
As it disappears into the distant
    horizon
Flowed sleepily
Into the stranger's bag.

The clear blue of the
Sparkling sky
Swirled into the stranger's cold bag
Like a tornado

The emerald green
Of the crystal grass
Ripped furiously from the ground
And into the dismal bag

A stranger left this afternoon.
He left behind a dismal place
And skipped happily along
To his colourful new world

By Alexandra Dearing, aged 9
Hatfield Woodhouse Primary School,
Doncaster
Yorks and Humberside Winner

The Stranger at the End Of the Rainbow ***

A stranger called this morning
Dressed all in black and grey
Put every colour in a bag
And carried them away.

The tongue tingling red of the strawberry ice lolly,
The lip smacking red of the girl
Walking ungracefully down the city.

The pumpkin's mouth orange colour
Glittering in the night.
Sunsets bright expressing themselves
Around the horizon.
Flaming phoenix growing from fire.

The eye melting green of the jealous monster
Dragging itself
Leaving mucus around the lime country.

The eye-catching silver of the moon's
Reflection
Melted in the ocean.

The stranger sat nervously at the end of the rainbow,
A sucking suitcase covered in colours.
And this is why
Colours exist.

By Akbar Zab, aged 9
Norbury Manor Primary School, Norbury, London

*** Teachers' National Awards for Improvement Winner
Akbar was born in Russia and lived in Ecuador before moving to England at the age of eight. Though fluent in Spanish and possessing some knowledge of Russian, Akbar knew only three words of English by the age of eight when he moved to the UK. In only one year he has achieved Level 3 in his Reading and Writing 'SATs ' and now he has composed this award-winning poem.

The Colour Collector ***

A stranger called this morning
Dressed all in black and grey,
Put every colour in a bag,
And carried them away.

The tongue tingling red of the strawberry ice lolly,
The red of sunburn burning on my back,
The bubbling red lava flowing from the volcano,
The red mark when you get a whack.

Grabbed the yellow from the soggy chips,
Took the brick yellow from the garden wall,
Stole the yellow from the juicy lemon,
Snatched the painful yellow from the bruise where I had a fall.

The pale purple from the piece of sugar paper,
The sweet purple from the juicy plum,
The shiny purple from the glass beads,
The passion fruit purple from the chewing gum.

Grabbed the rough green out of my squeaky alligator,
Took the bright green from the tree top leaves,
Stole the gentle green from the runner beans,
Snatched the delicious green from the freshly picked peas.

A stranger called this morning,
He didn't leave his name,
Left us only darkness,
Life will never be the same.

By Aaron Gratton, aged 9
Shawley County Primary School, Epsom
*** Teachers' National Awards for Improvement Winner
In the past, Aaron suffered from an inability to express himself in language, which
proved especially frustrating for him as he has always demonstrated a highly imaginative
nature. Through remarkable concentration and effort, however, Aaron has substantially
overcome this barrier.

FILM/TV SCRIPT

PHIL REDMOND WROTE ...

Scene 1

Luke's bedroom. Morning

Luke is lying in bed. He has the covers pulled tight up over his head. He can hear heavy footsteps on the stairs, then his brother Ben's voice as the door flies open.

Ben   Luke? Luke? Where are you?

Ben then slams the door behind him. Luke pops his head out from under the covers.

Luke   I'm here.

Ben   So is he. He's downstairs.

Luke   You mean he's really here?

Ben   Yes. *(But then he stops and listens. He has heard a noise)* Oh no. Let me get in.

Ben jumps under the bed covers.

Luke   Why?

Ben   Can't you hear? He's coming up the stairs.

Luke   Oh no!

The two boys quickly pull up the bed covers to hide ...

INTRODUCING THE
FILM AND TV SCRIPTS

Who, or what, was coming up the stairs?

Once our scriptwriters had the answer to that – and how their brains must have been teeming with possibilities – their film and TV treatments could take off. As it happens, seven of our nine winners chose to take flight into fantasy, making good use of the infinite flexibility of the form. They conjured genies, snow demons, ancestral ghosts, wizard relations, mad teachers and mysterious strangers.

In *The Holographic Parents* a mad science teacher turns the boys' parents into holograms who surf cyberspace intent on taking over the world. In *Voyage* the boys are whisked away to a desert, their task to find a missing jewelled sword guarded by a dragon. Both *Payback Time!* and *The Ghost That Lost His Hand* introduce the supernatural, chillingly in the form of a snow demon determined to make one of the boys a creature of the living-dead like himself, and comically when the boys find themselves on an historic French battleground hunting for a ghostly disembodied hand.

But you don't have to have wonderfully improbable adventures in far-flung places and other times; exciting things can happen at home. Why not, for instance, bring the most famous scientist of all, Albert Einstein, to the garden shed, as our scriptwriters did in *The Day We Blew Up the Toaster*? They want his help in building an amazing, multifunctioning toaster to replace the one the boys blew up. (You have to be bold to grab the producer's attention.) Or create eccentric, over-the-top relatives, such as Gran in *Operation Get Rid of Gran,* who still thinks she's seventeen and acts like it to the boys' acute embarrassment; or Uncle Blake, an incompetent wizard who makes the boys' school disappear by mistake (only Auntie Dot in Transylvania with her crystal ball can undo the damage).

And yet, two groups of scriptwriters remind us that there is just as much excitement to be had in realistic dramas. In *Outside School,* fast-moving scenes take us into derelict houses, a prison, even into the arms of a gang of bullies, as Jake, a friend of the boys, has bewildering encounters with his long-lost father; the shifts in Jake's thinking match the twists and turns of the plot. *The Blind Date* centres on the dramatic theme of bullying, a funny, streetwise treatment in a particularly fluent script that uses modern idioms well and has a nice line in sarcasm.

If these scripts give us a foretaste of the inventiveness of our future TV and film scriptwriters in the multi-channelled digital age, we're in for an entertaining roller-coaster ride.

The Ghost That Lost His Hand

Main characters
Ben, Luke, Ghost, Guards

Scene 1

Luke's bedroom. Morning

Ben	Can't you hear? He's coming up the stairs.
Luke	Oh no!

The two boys quickly pull up the bed covers to hide. A strange mist comes through the door.

Luke	What's that cloud?
Ben	Looks like a ghost to me.

The cloud starts to form into a human shape.

Luke	Maybe it is.
Ghost	*(Casually)* Don't be afraid, I am your ancestor.
Ben	*(Quivering)* What happened to your hand?
Ghost	It got cut off … so you will help get it back.
Luke	How was it cut off?
Ghost	It got cut off by the French Army.

Scene 2

A French battlefield

The children are transported back in time to France. They hear loud bangs and the cries of dying men.

Ben	How did we get here?
Ghost	Time line dimension.

Ben	What's your name, Mr Ancestor?
Ghost	Sir Drake Headwig.
Luke	So you come from Dad's side of the family?
Ghost	That's right.
	*An arrow skims over **Luke's** head.*
Luke	That was close.
Ben	*(He picks up a crossbow)* What's this?
Ghost	That's rare – it's a double-barrelled crossbow. Why don't you try it out?
Ben	How?
Luke	*(Sarcastically)* Pull the trigger.
	***Ben** pulls the trigger. They hear a noise.*
French Guard	*(In pain)* Aaahhh!
Luke	You pinned him to the drawbridge.
Ghost	Look, the bridge is lowering.
	There is a loud splashing noise.
Ben	The soldier had a good wash.
Ghost	Hurry up! We've got to get to the centre of France.

Scene 3

The centre of France

Ghost	To the execution chamber.
Luke	*(Whispering)* How do we get past the guards?
Ghost	With Ben's crossbow.
	***Ben** aims and fires.*

Guards 1 and 2	*(Loud cries of agony)* AAAHHH!
Ghost	Look for a glowing hand.
Luke	Here it is!
Ghost	Thank you, Luke.
	A light comes on. They are surrounded by hundreds of guards.
Luke and Ben	AAAHHH!
Captain	Guards, take them away.
Ghost	Luke, use your penknife. Ben, use your crossbow.
	They threaten the guards with their weapons.

Scene 4

A derelict house, later

Ghost	This looks familiar.
Ben and Luke	What, in a past life or something?
Ghost	Well, I am a ghost, I did have a life once. *(Looking at dusty pictures on the walls)* Do you think I share a resemblance to these portraits?
Ben	Well, they're all dead, aren't they?
	Ben *and* **Luke** *start laughing.*
Luke	I'm sure the pictures are looking at us!
	All of a sudden, a wind blows all the windows open.
Ghost	Ahhh! I'm getting sucked out! Your time must be getting to an end.
Ben	*(Looking at* **Luke***)* Look! My hands are vanishing! I don't want to be a ghost!
Luke	Neither do I! I want my tea, I'm hungry! But who were we following?
Ghost	It must be my ancestor, Sir Shining Armour. Give me my hand and all will be back to normal.
	The **ghost** *tries to grab the hand from* **Luke***.*
Luke	No, we will be left in the cloud for ever if we give you your hand.
	The cloud passes through the window.
Luke and Ben	Bye bye, Sir Drake Headwig.

Ghost	Thank you, thank you, but please, my hand …
Ben	Give it to him now.
	They pass over the hand and start praying.

Scene 5
Luke's bedroom

Ben	What happened?
Luke	Not sure. Give me time to think.
Ben	I'm hungry. Let's see what's for breakfast. I hope it's not fried snails!
	As they walk out of the room, a picture of a knight in armour moves.
Luke	Did you see that?
Ben	What?
Luke	Doesn't matter, it must be my imagination.

By Allan Bowman, aged 9
Scott Lawson, aged 10
Daniel Kelleher, aged 10
Layla Hawkins, aged 10

Princecroft Primary School, Warminster
South West Winners

Voyage

Main characters
Ben, Luke, a Stranger, a Genie

Scene 1

Luke's bedroom. Morning

Ben   Can't you hear? He's coming up the stairs.

Luke   Oh no!

The two boys quickly pull up the bed covers to hide ...

Ben   (Whispering) Is he in the room yet?

Luke   I don't know.

Ben   Let's keep quiet and listen for him.

The door opens with a creak.

Stranger Hello?

There's a sound like the smashing of a bottle. The boys feel themselves being whisked away.

Scene 2

The desert. Afternoon

They look down and see that they are dressed in desert clothes.

Ben   What's that?

He points to a piece of paper inside a bottle. For the first time, they notice they are not alone.

Stranger Ha ha, I've got you now!

Luke   Oh, no!

Ben	*(Grabbing the bottle)* Leg it, Luke!
	The boys run. A while later, they stop.
Luke	Open the bottle, Ben, and see what's inside!
	Ben *opens the bottle.*
Ben	This is what it says: 'If you want to get out of this mess, then you must try and complete this quest, find a genie and he will tell you what to do.'
Luke	There's something else in there, it's a map! *(They look at the map)* It tells us to go this way.
	He points to the left. The boys run until they find a cave. They decide to look inside.
Ben	Let's try in here!

Scene 3

The genie's cave. Evening

A voice booms through the cave.

Luke	Oh no!
Genie	Come here, young boy!
	*The **genie** points to **Ben**. Bravely, **Ben** walks forward.*
Ben	*(Gulping)* Er … we are here because …
	*Shakily he hands the **genie** the paper.*
Genie	Oh, I see. Well, if you want to get out of here, you must kill a dragon. To get to it, you must climb a mountain and there you will find its cave. You must kill it with a diamond-encrusted sword (which you will find in the sacred waterfall on the mountain also) and at the exact stroke of midnight. When you have killed it, come back here.
	With this, he disappears.

Scene 4

The mountain, later

Luke   *(Trembling)* What's that noise?

Ben   I don't know because I can't hear it. Come on. I can see the sacred waterfall.

Luke   I don't know, Ben …

Ben   Oh, don't be such a wimp!

All of a sudden, a huge tornado hits them. They fall into the sacred falls.

Luke   Aaahhh … told you, Ben! Ouch, what's this?

He pulls out the diamond sword.

Luke   Oh, it's only a sword.

He goes to throw it back into the water.

Ben   Stop! It's the diamond sword we need!

They pull themselves back onto the shore.

Luke   Now I guess all we need to find is that dragon's cave.

Ben   We don't need to look very far, do we? It's right in front of us!

Luke   Oh, come on, then.

Scene 5

Outside the cave, a few minutes later

Ben   Well, we are going to have to face the challenge now. Are you up for it?

Luke   Yes!

Ben   Here it goes!

They step inside the cave and swing the sword around their heads. They get a big surprise – a note and a red jewel are all that are in the cave. The note says the dragon has gone out and will be back shortly. Quickly they hurry out before the dragon gets back.

Ben   Now we have to go back to the genie.

Luke   Oh yeah.

Scene 6

Back at the genie's cave, very late

Ben   O Genie, we have done your deeds. Will you please tell us how to get home now?

Genie   *(Holding out a bottle)* Drink this, the next thing you know, you'll be home.

Ben   *(Drinking the mixture)* Ugh, disgusting!

Luke   *(Yawning)* He's asleep …

Scene 7

Luke's bedroom. Morning

*Luke wakes up and hears a person coming into his bedroom. It's **Ben**.*

Luke   Did you like the adventure last night?

Ben   What adventure?

Luke   You know!

Ben   What?

Luke   Oh, forget it. It was a dream.

Ben   Or was it?

By Laura Ward, aged 9
Sarah Kostrzewski, aged 9
Joshua Sawbridge, aged 8
Joanna Hassall, aged 9

Little Hill Primary School, Wigston
East Midlands Winners

Operation Get Rid Of Gran

Main characters
Ben, Luke, Dad, Gran, Miss Ding Dong, Mum

Scene 1

Luke's bedroom. Morning

Ben Can't you hear? He's coming up the stairs.

Luke Oh no!

The two boys quickly pull up the bed covers to hide ...

Dad Boys, I've got bad news. Your uncle couldn't make it so guess who's here to take care of you for three days?

Gran *(In a high squeaky voice)* Dearies! Oh, dearies!

Ben It's even worse!

Luke *(Whispering)* It's Gran!

Ben *(Whispering)* Remember what she did last year? She showed all our baby photos to the whole neighbourhood!

*Gran walks into **Luke** and **Ben's** room dressed in 17-year-old clothes, a belly top, hipsters, and leather knee-high boots. She pulls off the sheets.*

Luke and Ben	AAAGGGHHH!
Gran	*(In a high squeaky voice)* Oh how precious, you've grown a great deal since I last saw you, my little buttercup!
Ben	What on earth are you wearing?
Gran	Don't you think I look groovy, man?
Ben	*(Astonished)* Gran, you don't look groovy. You're seventy-three!
Luke	*(Convincingly)* No, Gran, you look more than groovy.
Gran	*(Excitedly)* Well, okay then.
	***Gran** leaves the room.*
Ben	*(Quickly jumping out of bed)* What did you say that for? Now she thinks we like what she's wearing!
	***Ben** and **Luke** get ready for school.*

Scene 2

At school

***Miss Ding Dong** is doing the register in **Luke** and **Ben's** class. The pupils just call her Miss.*

Miss	Simon?
Simon	Sandwiches ple …
	***Gran** bursts into the room.*
Gran	Hello, Miss Dong Ding!
Miss	It's Miss Ding Dong. You must be the new French teacher.
	***Gran** looks round, puzzled.*
Gran	Oh, dearies. You've forgotten your lunch again. What ya like?
	***Ben** and **Luke** go red in the face.*
Ben	*(Shouting)* GRAN!
Luke	What are you doing?
	***Gran** is chewing gum. She still looks puzzled.*
Gran	*(Coughing)* I'm ch-choking, HELP!
	***Luke** and **Ben** slap her on the back.*
Luke	There you go, Gran.
	*Her gum flies out of her mouth into **Miss Ding Dong's** hair.*
Miss	Aaahhh! Get it out, get it out!

Gran	Oh sorry, lovely. Well, got to run. Here's your sandwiches, boys. Oh by the way I'm making your favourite tonight *(rubbing her tummy)* – liver and onions.
Class	*(All screwing up their faces)* Errr!

Scene 3

Walking home from school

Luke	We must do something about Gran. She's everywhere we go.
Ben	I've got an idea. I'll tell you when we get in.
	Ben *and* ***Luke*** *run into their house and rush upstairs to* ***Luke's*** *room.*
Gran	*(Shouting)* Boys, I've got a surprise for you.
Ben	Not now Gran, we're doing our homework.
Luke	What's your idea, Brainy Box?
	Ben *whispers into* ***Luke's*** *ear.*
Luke	*(With lots of expression)* That's a great idea!

Scene 4

Night time. Pitch black

	Gran *is asleep and* ***Ben*** *and* ***Luke*** *are just coming out of* ***Luke's*** *room.*
Ben	*(Whispering)* Are you ready?
Luke	Let's go for it!
	Ben *and* ***Luke*** *tiptoe into* ***Gran's*** *room. They are dressed up as ghosts, wearing old sheets.*
Luke and Ben	*(Spookily)* Whooo! Aaggnness!
Gran	*(Suddenly waking up. Shaking)* W-what do you w-want from m-me?
Luke and Ben	*(Loudly and spookily)* Whooooo! Don't let what happened to me happen to you!
Gran	*(Puzzled and scared)* What happened? Who are you?
Luke	*(Spookily)* Whoooooo, leave this place, Agnes, NOW!
Ben	I'm only trying to warn you!
Gran	What? What will happen?
Ben	Just leave now! Whooo!
Gran	AAAGGGHHH!

	Ben *and* **Luke** *leave the room.* **Gran** *rings their parents.*
Gran	*(Sounding scared)* Quickly, come back home, your house is full of ghosts and they know my name, aaaggghhh!
	Gran *hangs up, before their parents can say anything.*

Scene 5

Morning. Gran has packed her bags

Parents walk through door.

Gran	Ghosts! Ghosts! They're everywhere. I've been up all night guarding my best possessions. Run, run, save yourselves!

Gran *runs out of the house.*

Gran	Taxi, taxi!

She jumps in a taxi.

Mum	What's all that about?
Luke	Let's just say Gran's got an active imagination!

By Rebecca Lloyd, aged 10
Ruth Barraclough, aged 10
Lucy Bedford, aged 10
Catherine Longbottom, aged 10

Towngate School, Wakefield
Yorks and Humberside Winners

The Blind Date*

Main characters

Ben, Luke, Amy, Marcus, Rob, Dave and Joe

Scene 1

Luke's bedroom. Morning

Ben	Can't you hear? He's coming up the stairs.
Luke	Oh no!

The two boys quickly pull up the bed covers to hide ...

Ben	*(In an urgent whisper)* I don't believe he actually came! He believed it!
Luke	It's your fault – you sent the e-mail.
Ben	But you wrote it.
Luke	It was your idea.
Ben	Shh! He's nearly on the landing.
Luke	Oh why did we ever start this?
Ben	Because he's a bully who needs teaching a lesson.
Luke	But what will *she* do when she finds out what we've done?
Ben	Kill us, probably, but it'll be worth it to see his face! Now shush!

Scene 2

The landing

Marcus – the bully – reaches the top of the stairs. He's carrying flowers. He calls the name of the girl he thinks he's arranged to see this morning for a day out together. A sleepy voice calls out from a bedroom.

Marcus	Amy, Amy, are you there? It's Marcus. You said nine o'clock ...
Amy	Marcus? *(Quietly to herself)* Marcus who? Not that ninny from school. What would he be doing here on a Saturday morning, or any morning come to that! Wait a minute! Luke and Ben! Those brothers ... it must be! *(Thinking quickly, she calls out)* Not quite ready. Could you wait downstairs a mo?

Marcus	Of course … whatever you say … straight away.
	Marcus goes downstairs to wait for his 'date'. Amy storms into the boys' room.

Scene 3

Luke's bedroom

Ben	*(Before Amy can say anything)* We can explain!
Amy	You'd better. What on earth?
Luke	It was his idea. He said we could make Marcus pay for bullying the Year Sevens by showing him up.
Ben	It was his idea. I only went along because someone needs to stop Marcus making their lives so unbearable, and we know he fancies you like mad, so …
Amy	So you thought you'd set up a fake date with me? I sussed that was what you'd done. And what now? What was supposed to happen now, geniuses?
Ben	Aren't you mad at us?
Amy	I should be, but you're right, he needs taking down some. So, like I said, what now?
Luke	Phew! I think I was more scared of you than him! Thanks, sis. We haven't really thought what next. I guess we never thought he'd turn up!
Amy	Well he has, so let's get thinking. I'll get rid of him for now, tell him I've got a headache and I'll ring him later … something or other. Now you two, we need a plan.

Scene 4

Outside the cinema, in the evening

Marcus is standing outside the cinema, carrying a bunch of roses. He's waiting to take Amy to see a romantic film. One by one his friends arrive – Amy has texted them pretending to be Marcus, arranging to see the latest wrestling movie at the same cinema.

Rob	Hi Marcus. Are the others here yet?
Marcus	*(Hiding the roses behind his back)* Rob? What are you doing here?
Rob	Ha ha! I can't wait to see this film. D'you think we'll get in? It's an eighteen. My mum thinks I've come to see that sad film with Leonardi da Vinci in it … as if!
Marcus	*(Blushing)* Yeah … as if.
Dave	Yo, dudes, ready for some serious Tombstones?

Joe	Whodaman! Marcy dude, what's with the clothes? You look like you're going to Sunday School, not wrestling!
Marcus	*(To himself)* What's going on? Why are the guys all here? And where's Amy got to?
Rob	Come on, it's time to go in. What'ya waiting for?
Marcus	You go ahead … I'll be in in a second.

*An hour and a half later, the boys come out. **Marcus** is sitting on the pavement, squashed roses by his side.*

Joe	Hey Marcus, you missed a seriously bad movie. What happened?

***Marcus** stands up, looks at his mates, and tries to decide whether to tell them he's been stood up and look an idiot, or try to think of a good excuse for sitting on the pavement for an hour and a half with a bunch of crushed flowers. Just then, **Amy** comes round the corner. **Marcus** looks relieved and runs up to her.*

Marcus	Amy! I knew there'd be a reason. It's okay, I understand, something must have come up … we can still have some time together.
Amy	*(Looking seriously puzzled)* I beg your pardon? Are you talking to me? Do you suffer from the delusion that I would ever consider going out with *you*, or even share this planet with you if I had the choice? Bullies are just *so* uncool.

***Marcus** is left bright red with his mouth wide open as **Amy** walks away, head high. His friends collapse in a heap, laughing at him and imitating **Amy's** put-down.*

Scene 5

Just around the corner, near the cinema

***Luke** and **Ben** finish videoing the scene. They high-five.*

Luke and Ben	Mission accomplished!
Ben	Yeah, and next time he bullies someone, guess what will be substituted for the assembly video?

They walk off together smiling.

By Kathryn Snook, aged 10
Olive Gana, aged 10
Charlotte Drysdale, aged 9
Jane Roberts-Davies, aged 10

Bentley Heath Primary School, Solihull
West Midlands Winners
* National Winner

Payback Time!

Main characters
Ben, Luke, Dan (a ghost)

Scene 1

Luke's bedroom. Morning

Ben Can't you hear? He's coming up the stairs.

Luke Oh no!

The two boys quickly pull up the bed covers to hide. The door flies open and an icy blast chills the whole room. Out of a tornado of cold mist emerges a tall white figure.

Luke It's Dan, isn't it?

Ben You're right – it is.

Luke You know what they say – that ghosts always return on the anniversary of their death.

Ben *(Whispering)* It must have happened then?

Luke Yes it has, he's been captured and turned into a snow demon himself!

Dan *(Smirking)* Never make anything up about a ghost *ever* or you will get paid back horribly.

Luke *(Shaking uncontrollably with fright)* So was it really the snow demon who pushed you in the river and killed you last winter?

Dan I'm afraid it was. I made up a ghost in my imagination and spread the story of it to scare people but the ghost came true. Every year a snow demon has to be replaced and the old one is led to another dimension and lost in it for ever.

   ***Dan** floats towards **Luke**.*

Dan *(Whispering in **Luke's** ear)* If you go down to the river at seven o'clock you will find a secret hiding place where I used to keep my treasures when I was little. If you go down to the place where I died you will find a large rock with my initials carved on it. Then dig underneath the rock – but do not take Ben!

Scene 2

At the river at seven o'clock

Luke is at the river, searching for the rock. As he steps forward to the water's edge, he realises why Dan has told him to go down to the river. Dan wants to kill Luke to make him the new snow demon and then be lost in another dimension for ever. Just as Luke turns to run away, Dan pushes him in the river.

Luke   *(Faintly)* Aaahhh! I thought you were my friend!

Scene 3

Back at the house, in the garden. Eight o'clock

Ben   I wonder where Luke is? Maybe he's gone out with Dan to the river or maybe he's gone out to the playing fields. I'll try the river. Oh no! What if ...

Scene 4

Back at the river

Ben sprints to the river. He sees Luke's body floating in the water. Ben dives in to try and save his brother but Luke is stone cold.

Ben   Nooo!

Then he hears Dan behind him.

Dan   Fooled ya! You and your brother are stupid enough to think that I won't kill you because you were there when I died – and did you do much about it? No!

Ben   I thought I could trust you.

Dan   Do you know what?

Ben   What?

Dan   I think your brother is going to kill you!

Dan explodes into a ball of snow, then Luke appears where Dan was standing. Luke is now a ghost.

Ben   Is it true then? Are you going to kill me like Dan killed you?

Luke doesn't answer but Ben guesses what he is thinking.

The End?

By Louise Young, aged 10
Chantelle Fairburn, aged 10
Olivia Liddle, aged 10

Stanhope Primary School, South Shields
North East Winners

Blake's Magical Mistake

Main characters

Ben, Luke, Uncle Blake, Miss Cooper, Mrs Jones, Auntie Dot

Scene 1

Luke's bedroom. Morning

*A letter has arrived from **Uncle Blake**, saying he's coming on an unexpected visit.*

Ben Can't you hear? He's coming up the stairs.

Luke Oh no!

The two boys quickly pull up the covers to hide ...

Uncle Blake *(Silently opening the door)* There's no use hiding, I've always been good at hide and seek.

He points his wand at the bed cover which all at once rises up to the ceiling.

Ben and Luke Aaahhh!

Uncle Blake *(Puzzled)* What's going on, didn't your father tell you I was coming?

Ben and Luke Y-y-you're a w-wizard!

Uncle Blake What! Didn't you know? Oh never mind that. You'd better hurry up or you'll be late for school.

***Uncle Blake** walks the children to school.*

Scene 2

At school

Uncle Blake is hiding in a bush, trying to hear what Ben and Luke are saying. Miss Cooper walks past.

Ben and Luke	Hi, Miss Cooper.
Miss Cooper	*(Angrily)* Why are you here so early? Because you've broken one of the school rules, you've earned yourselves a detention.
Ben	I hate that Miss Cooper!
Luke	Yeah, she's a real pain giving us detention. I wish she would disappear.

Uncle Blake, still hiding in the bush, hears them.

Uncle Blake	Your wish is my command.

Uncle Blake points his wand at Miss Cooper and does a spell.

Uncle Blake	Kongo, bongo, banish, manish, make this stupid old hag vanish!

A blue beam comes out of the wand and is going to hit Miss Cooper. She bends down to tie her shoelace and the blue beam misses her and hits the school. It vanishes!

Uncle Blake	Oops!

The children see Uncle Blake and walk over to him.

Uncle Blake	*(Looking at the sky)* W-what a … um, lovely day it is.
Ben and Luke	Uncle *Blaaake!*

The school bus arrives and the children crowd around in the playground. Mrs Jones, the headteacher, enters and sees that the school is missing.

Mrs J	Huh?

Everything is silent, and all of a sudden the playground erupts. All the children skip and run and shout that the school has gone. Adults and bystanders stare and wonder what's going on.

Mrs J	*(In shock)* Where is my lovely beautiful school? It's gone, gone, gone.
Miss C	I don't know what happened. One minute it was here, then it had disappeared.
Mrs J	I must phone the police. Everybody may as well go home, there's nothing to see. Miss Cooper, can I use your mobile?

Scene 3

Outside where the school was, later

*The police are questioning **Mrs Jones** and other teachers. A news van from Channel Five arrives.*

News Reporter 1	Welcome to Coopers Lane School, or shall I call it Pragnell Road, because Coopers Lane School has disappeared!
News Reporter 2	It's amazing how the school suddenly just disappeared. How will we find out about what happened? It's magic. Where will the kids go to now that the school has gone?

Scene 4

At home, Ben is watching television

Ben	*(Shouting)* Uncle Blake, Luke, look – they're talking about the vanished school. It's a news flash.
Luke	Really, you mean it's on TV?
Ben	Come quick, Mrs Jones is on.

__Luke__ and __Uncle Blake__ walk into the living room.

Luke	Oh no, now what are we going to do?
Uncle Blake	Wait, maybe I could ... no ... Or maybe I could ... no, that won't work.

He shakes his head.

Uncle Blake	Or maybe. No.
Luke	Forget it. I don't want you to make it worse.
Ben	Just forget it, our lives are over.
Uncle Blake	Look on the bright side – at least you don't have to do any more school work or detentions.
Luke	Yeah.
Ben	But what are we going to do at home?
Luke	I really like school.
Ben	We'll miss all our friends.
Luke and Ben	We don't want to go to another school. We're happy where we are.

__Uncle Blake__ looks very guilty and turns away from the children.

Scene 5

In Transylvania

Dot   I must see what Blake is doing in England. I do hope he is having a really good time with his family. Let's hope he hasn't made a mess of things. I remember when he transformed a rare plant into a rose and I could not change it back.

She picks up her crystal ball from the table and says a spell.

Dot   Crystal, crystal, crystal ball, you are the cleverest one of them all. Please show me Blake with his family and friends, through your round and shiny lens.

Dot sees the chaos Blake has caused in the crystal ball.

Dot   Oh fiddlesticks, what has he done now? I'll have to go over there.

Dot snaps her fingers and is transported to Luke and Ben's house.

Scene 6

In Luke and Ben's house

Dot   You nincompoop, you're always doing things wrong. Wait till I get you home.

Uncle Blake   It wasn't my fault. My wand backfired on me.

Ben and Luke   He didn't mean to. He was only trying to help us.

Dot   Oh dear, oh dear!

Boys and U. Blake   Could you please reverse the spell?

Dot   *(Muttering)* Oh well, all right then, but we'll have to go back when it's dark.

Scene 7

Later that night, at the school

Luke   I hope it works.

Ben   Yeah, it's funny but I even missed doing maths today.

Dot   Don't worry, boys, it's a perfect night for my spell. Now keep out of my way. Blake, let this be a lesson to you.

Uncle Blake   Yes, dear.

Luke and Ben   Good luck, Auntie Dot!

Dot	Stupid Blake has ruined the school, please turn it back so it seems normal. Make teachers happy, no more jibes, let the children have the time of their lives.
	*Rewind film and freeze it before **Blake** does his accidental spell on the school.*

Scene 8

The next morning

Luke, Ben, Blake and Dot walk to school. The boys are very excited.

Dot	Now remember. I added some magic into my spell so nobody will remember any of the events that happened yesterday. That will be our little secret.
	***Blake** and **Dot** leave and **Miss Cooper** arrives.*
Luke	*(Groaning)* Oh no!
Miss C	*(Smiling)* Hello, boys, what a lovely day it is.
Luke and Ben	*(Looking at each other)* Eh?
Miss C	Come with me, boys.
Ben	*(Sighing)* Here we go again, hello detention.
	***Miss Cooper** leads them to the playground where they discover ...*
Luke	*(Gasping)* Wow! A *fairground!*
	The children arrive in the school bus and cheer tumultuously for the school and all the teachers. Scene ends with children and staff of school going on the fairground, happy and laughing.

By Richard Archer, aged 10   Alexander Arden, aged 10
David Ashdown, aged 10   Harry Barnard, aged 10
Katherine Broad, aged 10   Jack Brown, aged 10
Gemma Carby, aged 10   Chantal Chea, aged 10
Benjamin Crawshaw, aged 9   Laurie Davis, aged 10
Bimpe Fashanu, aged 10   Joshua Friskey, aged 10
Luke Gilby, aged 10   Georgina Hart, aged 9
Joseph Harvey, aged 10   Bobbie Hilton, aged 10
Olufemi Kaseram, aged 10   Michael McLeary, aged 10
Hayley Mills, aged 10   Laura-Anne Moss, aged 9
George Osbourne, aged 10   Luke Patmore, aged 10
Roshanne Powell, aged 9   Kerrie Scott, aged 9
Catherine Sharp, aged 10   Christopher Turner, aged 10
Leigh-Ann Walkerdine, aged 10   Jamie Warrington, aged 10

Coopers Lane Primary School, Lewisham
London Winners

The Holographic Parents

Main characters
Ben, Luke, Mum, Dad, Mad Scientist, Egor

Scene 1

Luke's bedroom. Morning

Ben	Can't you hear? He's coming up the stairs.
Luke	Oh no!
	The two boys quickly pull up the bed covers to hide. Mum comes in with a pile of ironing
Mum	Luke, Ben, where are you? It's time for your science open day.
Ben and Luke	We're just coming, Mum.
Dad	*(Shouting from the front door)* You'd better hurry up or we'll be late.

Scene 2

Fifteen minutes later, at school

Mum	That must be your science teacher. Let's go out and meet him.
Luke and Ben	Dad, can we go and have a look at our friends' experiments?
Dad	Yep! Sure you can, we'll be over here talking to your science teacher.
Mad Scientist	*(Speaking in a French accent)* Hello, you must be Mr and Mrs Bogg. I am the guide for today. The science teacher of your children.
Mum	What shall we call you then?
Mad Scientist	You may call me ze mad zientist.

*Suddenly a strange looking human comes from behind a wall behind the **Mad Scientist**.*

Egor	You called, master?
Mad Scientist	*(Speaking in a mysterious voice)* Take them into the back room and sit them down.
Parents	Um … excuse me, but I don't think you have introduced us to him.
Mad Scientist	Oh, I almost forgot.
Mum	You did forget.
Mad Scientist	*(Chuckling)* Yes, quite right. His name is Egor.

***Egor**, **Mum** and **Dad** go into the back room which has got tons of strange pieces of machinery and tools in it.*

Egor	Sit down.

***Mum** and **Dad** sit down and then suddenly some leg and arm clamps clamp them down.*

Egor	Ha, ha, ha you are now going to die.

*He picks up two strange helmets which are attached to a strange machine and puts them on **Mum** and **Dad**. A strange bolt of lightning-like substance goes through a tube which is attached to the helmets. **Mum** and **Dad** become holographic.*

Egor	I am now going to shut down so that you can't reverse the process.

***Egor** temporarily shuts down. The clamps unclamp and **Mum** and **Dad** get up to look around.*

Holographic Dad	Man, I feel powerful, maybe we can do something bad. I wish we were home.

116

Scene 3

At home

*The next second they are at home, **Holographic Dad** lying on the couch.*

H Dad   WHOA!

H Mum   If we just did that, we might be able to do anything. Maybe if we surf cyberspace we can appear in a computer somewhere else. Then we can take over the world!

H Dad   You're jumping to conclusions.

H Mum   Come on, stop being a party pooper! It will be fun.

H Dad   Okay! Okay! Let's get access to the cyberspace pass.

They both click their fingers and they travel through cyberspace, some planets flying towards them.

Scene 4

At school

***Luke** and **Ben** are wandering around looking for their parents. In the science lab they find **Egor** the robot. They put **Egor** back on line.*

Egor   Your mum and dad will take over the world for my master. Beam me up, Scottie.

*   **Egor** gets teleported to an alien spaceship in the Omega region. **Ben** and **Luke** surf the Internet.*

Luke   Look at this, Ben. Nuclear missiles have been stolen and continents are being destroyed. Do you think it is Mum and Dad?

Ben   Probably, but we can't go into the country that they are in.

Luke   They'll go home soon for a rest. Come on!

Scene 5

At home

***Ben** and **Luke** go home, they find their parents and try to talk to them. But they don't listen and tie up the boys. **Egor** appears.*

Egor   Oya, oya, oya, oya!

*   **Egor** unties **Luke** and **Ben**. But then **Egor** gets tied to a rocket by **Holographic Mum** and **Holographic Dad**.*

Egor   I will be back!

*The rocket ignites and **Egor** flies to the moon.*

Ben   Mum, Dad, come with us.

Luke	We can give you more power than you can ever imagine!
H Mum and H Dad	Really?

Ben and Luke take their parents to the lab.

Scene 6

Back at the lab

Luke	Put on these helmets.

Holographic Mum and Dad put on the helmets. Ben turns a lever and Mum and Dad are back to normal.

Mum	What happened?
Luke and Ben	It doesn't matter. As long as you're back.

By   Helen Smith, aged 9
Faye Naul, aged 10
Jenny Dillon, aged 10
Bernard Hay, aged 10
Adam Carrington-Porter, aged 9

Mottram St Andrews Primary School, Macclesfield
North West Winners

The Day We Blew Up the Toaster

Main characters

Ben, Luke, Dad, Mum, Albert Einstein

Scene 1

Luke's bedroom, Saturday morning

Ben	Can't you hear? He's coming up the stairs.
Luke	Oh no!

*The two boys quickly pull up the bed covers to hide as the door flies open to reveal a very angry man who just happens to be **Luke** and **Ben's** dad.*

Dad	*(Absolutely fuming)* WHO BLEW UP THE TOASTER?

The boys peep out from under the covers.

Ben	*(Meekly)* We don't know. Have you asked the gerbils?
Luke	Or the goldfish?
Dad	*(Dangerously)* Gerbils and goldfish don't blow up toasters but annoying boys like you do!
Luke	You sure?
Dad	OF COURSE I'M SURE!

*The bedroom is like a sauna. Enter **Mum**.*

Mum	Everything all right, dear?
Dad	*(With gritted teeth)* Fine, Molly dear! Just fine!

*They argue. **Dad** turns around. **Luke** and **Ben** are gone.*

Dad	NNOOO!

Scene 2

The garden shed

Luke and Ben shiver in the corner of the garden shed. They had abseiled down the vines as Mum and Dad argued.

Luke	*(Agitated) Now* what do we do?
Ben	We could build a new toaster.
Luke	With this junk? *(He points to the garden tools)*
Ben	What we need is a miracle!

*Suddenly they hear a thump on the garden shed door. The boys freeze. They hear a voice. The door opens and **Albert Einstein** is standing there with his glasses hanging off the end of his nose. He looks a bit puzzled.*

Albert	*(Mumbling)* Got to work on that.
Luke	Who are you?
Albert	Albert Einstein is the name. E=MC2 + 67222.87
Ben	So miracles *do* happen.
Albert	So what is your problem?
Luke	Can you build a toaster?
Albert	One of those new-fangled things? Maybe. Show me one.
Ben	We would show you one but we … er … blew our one up … so you couldn't … er … start from scratch?
Albert	I'll try!

Scene 3

At the B&Q warehouse

*Four streets away, **Ben**, **Luke** and **Albert** are looking at toasters in the B&Q warehouse. **Albert** looks especially interested as he has never seen a modern toaster before.*

Ben	Whatever you do, Albert, don't stick your finger in them.
Albert	I'm not that stupid.

*Luke and Ben go off to look at other toasters leaving **Albert** alone. **Albert** is careful not to stick his finger in but instead he takes it apart. He gets lots of strange looks but he doesn't care and hums along merrily to himself. Later on he gets a bit bored and starts looking around. He trips over a lawnmower and falls head first into a shelf of paint. **Ben** and **Luke** apologise and drag him out of the store.*

Scene 4

In the car park

Luke	What was that for?
Albert	It's not my fault that the lawnmower was in the way. You know how absentminded I can be.
Ben	Did you get bored with the toasters? I think they are really interesting. I was fiddling with the timeswitch and that's how I blew our one up.
Albert	Did your toaster blow up into millions of pieces? Screws and all?
Luke and Ben	Yes.
Albert	Then I could fix it.
Luke	You can't fix that! It's beyond repair!
Albert	I have an idea! Back to the shed!
Shop Assistant	Get back here!

Scene 5

Back in the shed

Ben	So what's this big idea then?
Albert	I could use some of this junk you've got in here to build an even better toaster!
Luke and Ben	Can we help?
Albert	Sure!

Scene 6

A few days later, outside the shed

Luke, Ben and Albert watch Mum and Dad gasp in amazement at the new invention – a sit-on toaster with a built-in vending machine and coffee-maker. Unfortunately Dad faints before he can get a proper look.

Mum It's wonderful. I'm very glad you did blow up the toaster after all.

Ben *(Winking at Luke)* So are we.

Mum Why?

Luke Because it also has a few other surprises along with it …

By Samad Azad, aged 10
   Samuel Gebbett, aged 10
   Nicky Lee Saunders, aged 10
   Martin Falder, aged 10

   Stifford Primary School, Grays
   East of England Winners

Outside School

Main characters

Ben, Luke, Jake, Jake's dad, Policewoman, Gangleader

Scene 1

Luke's bedroom. Morning

Ben	Can't you hear? He's coming up the stairs.
Luke	Oh no!
	The two boys quickly pull up the bed covers to hide. The door opens.
Jake	Found ya!
Ben	This is getting boring, let's go to the clubhouse.
Luke	Good idea.

Scene 2

At the clubhouse (a wrecked house)

Luke	Brought the biscuits?
Ben	Yeah … Give us a can, Jake!
Jake	*(Whispering)* Quiet! Did ya hear something?
	They hear a thump.
Jake	You must've heard that!
Luke	Look! The door's shut – we left it open!
Ben	*(Getting worried)* There's someone in the house!
Luke	Jake, have a look!
Jake	Wimps! Probably just the wind. AAAHHH! HELP! HEL …
Ben and Luke	*(Looking at each other in disbelief)* Jake!
	*They hear the door slam, then they run down the stairs after **Jake**.*
Ben	*(Panicking)* Whoever he is, he's got away, I can't see him!
Luke	There he is – down there – follow him!
	They follow the mystery person through a dark, winding alley into the basement of another old wrecked house.

Scene 3

In the basement

Luke	*(Whispering)* There he is. *(He gasps for breath)* There's Jake.
Ben	*(Whispering)* I'll go untie him.
Luke	*(Whispering)* Good idea.
Mystery Person	Who's there? C'mon – show yourself!

Luke comes forward, Jake and Ben back away.

Luke	Who are you?... And what do you want?
M Person	That I cannot tell you. But who are you?
Luke	My name is Luke Ashford. *(He pauses)* If you want money *(He rummages through his pocket)* I've only got £1.52.
M Person	I don't want your money.
Jake	*(Recovering)* Then what *do* you want?

Ben runs to the window, opens it and calls for help. The Mystery Person shoves him out the way and runs out of the door. Four days later, the boys return to the basement, suspecting that the Mystery Person has burgled Ben and Luke's house.

Jake	*(Whispering)* There he is!
Ben	*(Whispering)* Look! There's my stuff.
Jake	*(Whispering)* Let's get it.
M Person	What do you want?
Luke	The police are on their way.

The Mystery Person runs off and leaves the bag behind.

Luke	Well, at least we've got our stuff!
Ben	Hey! What was all that about the police coming?
Luke	Oh! Just to frighten him!

They laugh.

Jake	*(Putting his fists up)* I could have had him – I could have, you know!
Ben	*(Slowly)* Jake ...
Jake	What?
Luke	Jake, look! There's a picture of you and your father in this bag!
Ben	What's that doing there?
Jake	This is getting complicated, let's go to the clubhouse.

Scene 4

At the clubhouse

M Person What are you doing here?

Luke More like what are *you* doing here?

Ben This is our clubhouse.

Jake Why have you got that picture of me and my father?

*The **Mystery Person** takes off his balaclava.*

M Person Because I'm your father.

*There is the sound of police cars and voices in the background but everything else is quiet. The police take **Jake's father** away. He reaches out for **Jake**, but **Jake** backs away with a mean look on his face.*

Scene 5

Jake's house, two days later

Ben Why didn't you help your father, Jake?

Luke Yeah! He's obviously into you.

Jake Why should I? He was the one who left me when I was only a year old. He didn't care about me – and he still doesn't. Otherwise he would have come back to me and Mum a long time ago!

Ben He's got a point …

Luke I can't believe you're even suggesting Jake's right; I thought you were with me!

Jake Oh, so you came to gang up on me then?

Ben No. We just want you to be happy.

Jake No you don't!

Luke JUST TALK TO HIM, BEN!

Jake Don't shout at me!

They walk off in a huff.

Scene 6

A prison cell

Jake Hi! *(pause)* Dad.

Dad Jake! How are you? I've missed you so much!!

Jake Me too … huh!

Scene 7

The clubhouse

Jake	Hi.
Luke	Uh – hi.
Jake	Where's Ben?
Luke	Getting some drinks.
Ben	Oh – hi.
Jake	Hi.
Ben	Look, I am so sorry.
Luke	No, I'm the one who should be sorry.
Jake	I went to see Dad!
Luke	Did you? How was he?
Jake	Fine ... do you want to go see him, like together?
Luke and Ben	Yeah, sure.

*But **Jake's dad** escapes from prison.*

Scene 8

The clubhouse

Jake	Dad! (***Jake*** *hugs him*)
Dad	Jake!
Jake	What are you doing here?
Dad	I came to see you!
Luke	What, you escaped from prison just to see Jake?
Dad	Yes and no. I did come to see Jake, but I also came to be free!
Ben	But aren't the police looking for you?
Dad	No! They'll hardly know I'm gone – 'cos I've only just been sentenced.
Jake	Why don't you stay at our place?
Dad	I'm leaving soon ...

He gets up with his luggage and sets off. They hear a vehicle screech.

Luke	I wonder what's happened?
Ben	Yeah, let's look.

Scene 9

In the road

They walk outside and rummage through a crowd of people gathering around a lorry.

Luke   What's happened?

Police-woman   This lorry has just hit him.

Ben   Is he unconscious?

Police-woman   Yes ... he is.

*They watch as the ambulance drives **Jake's dad** away. Later that week, **Jake's dad** dies.*

Scene 10

The clubhouse

Ben   What's so important, Luke, that we had to have an urgent meeting?

Luke   Jake's run away.

Ben   You're kidding!

Luke   No. His father died.

Ben   Oh. That must be tough on him.

Luke   Yeah. Where do you think he's gone?

Ben   Um ... Maybe his old house, he always wanted to live there again.

Scene 11

Jake's old house, the garden

Luke   He's not here – let's go.

Ben   Where else could he be?

They start to go home when some boys surround them.

Gangleader   *(Sarcastically)* Hello, hello, what have we got here then? Looks like some little boys – what's the matter? Lost your way home?

Ben   No, we've come to ... *(**Luke** nudges **Ben** hard to stop)*

Luke   To meet our friends actually.

Jake   Guys – what are you doing here?

Ben   Jake, there you are!

Gangleader   You know these guys, Jake?

Jake	Yeah – they're my-my-my *(Stutters as he's sees the look on the gang's faces)*
Gangleader	Your what?
Jake	My ex-friends.
Gangleader	Well, what are you doin' standing there – get rid of 'em!
Luke	What are you talking about? We're Jake's best friends, aren't we, Jake?
Gangleader	C'mon, don't just stand there, hit 'em!
Jake	*(**Jake** hits **Luke** and he falls to the ground bleeding)* Sorry!
Ben	Luke! Jake, what did you do that for? We're only worried.
	*Jake runs away with the gang. **Ben** gets **Luke** up. A moment later, **Jake** comes running up with plasters.*
Jake	Here, for Luke. Look, I'm so sorry. I don't know what has got into me. It's like ever since I've met those boys, I've changed.
Ben	How did you get involved with them, then?
Jake	Oh. I bumped into them running here and because I was so upset, and I needed company, I hung out with them.
Ben	Why don't you come home?
Jake	Everyone will be mad at me for running away – and I just can't face home!
Ben	No one will be mad at you, come on!
	They walk to the garden gate.

Scene 12

The road

Gangleader	Well, well, look at this. It's Jake and his ex-friends.
Jake	They're not my ex-friends, they're my best friends!
Gangleader	Well in that case, you're our ex-friend and you know what we do to ex- friends!
	*They hear police car sirens coming towards them and then stop. The gang run off and the police take **Ben**, **Jake** and **Luke** away. The boys try to explain that they didn't do anything but the police don't listen.*

By Aimée Breslin, aged 10
Suki Notay, aged 10

Whitehill Junior School, Gravesend
South East Winners